ON
ODYSSEY

A Memoir

MARION KENNEALLY

outskirtspress

DENVER, COLORADO

One Nun's Odyssey
A Memoir
All Rights Reserved.
Copyright © 2016 Marion Kenneally
v3.0

Outskirts Press, Inc.
http://www.outskirtspress.com

ISBN: 978-1-4787-6618-6

Library of Congress Control Number: 2015917979

Outskirts Press and the "OP" logo are trademarks belonging to Outskirts Press, Inc.

PRINTED IN THE UNITED STATES OF AMERICA

This book is dedicated to the memory of
my mother, Marion, who gave me life
and to
my father, Leo P. Kenneally,
who
inspired me to write

Table of Contents

Acknowledgments

I express my gratitude to my wife, Anna M. Bissonnette, for reading my manuscript and giving me feedback. I am deeply appreciative of the advice and suggestions from Susan Freireich, Michael Kirschenbaum, Barbara Kivowitz, Susan Landry, and Melissa Shook, members of my writing group.

I wish to thank Barbara Mende, Barbara Beckwith, Paul and Suzanne Pemsler, Kathleen Spivack, Bonnie Capes, Carol Hartman, Arlyn Schneider, Paula Maute, Mary Bonina, cousin Vaughan Rachel, and cousin Ken Dooley for their assistance, The Joiner Center at UMASS, Boston, and especially Lady Borton.

I thank Kerry Eielson and John Fanning of La Muse Writers' Retreat in La Bastide Esparbairenque, France.

Preface

"The only journey is the one within."
—*Rainer Maria Rilke*

In 1952, at the age of eighteen, I entered a semi-clois-tered order of teaching nuns in Fall River, Massachusetts. The mission of the nineteenth-century order, founded in northern France, was to buttress the teaching of secular subjects with Catholic doctrine and morals. In 1860, a small group of French and Irish nuns from the order came to America to establish a boarding school for girls in the mill town of Fall River.

In the summer of 1946, I read a novel about a young girl who attended a Catholic boarding school staffed by French nuns. In the story the sprinkling of foreign words such as *congé* (vacation) and *goûter* (afternoon tea) whet-ted my appetite and I hungered for more of the exotic lan-guage. Girls playing croquet on the manicured lawns—my imagination went into overdrive as I conjured up a kind of school utopia—perpetual play and camaraderie. I pictured the school's stately building, set high on a hill amid green-carpeted meadows and enclosed by fleur-de-lis wrought-iron fencing.

My greatest desire that summer was to go to a boarding school like the one in *A Year to Grow*. I besieged my parents, and finally in August my mother said we might have a look at the Fall River boarding school that a cousin had attended.

Thus began my fate. From first sight of the tall Victorian brick building encompassed by the wrought-iron fence, I was entranced. It is incomprehensible to me now that as a burgeoning teenager (I was twelve) I could have been so charmed by the institutional setting. What I did not know then was that my year at the Sacred Hearts Academy would be a harbinger of things to come.

This then is the story of my sixteen years in the convent—what motivated me to choose the life, why I stayed despite personal struggles, and what impelled me, finally, to seek a dispensation from my vows.

The story is true with the exception of some name changes to protect identities. In some cases I've left the original names when I was sure nothing could be construed as negative. It is my personal story. As the poet Homer said, "The journey is the thing."

The Ceremony

Sister Rosalie smiled as she slipped the veil over my head, pins in her mouth, her face close to mine as she fastened my starched collar. Each time her hands touched me, each time she bent over me, I got goose bumps. Her breath like mint, her ruby lips, and the scent of cedar on her clothes—these sensations were as fresh to me as they'd been on that day five years earlier when I'd fallen in love with her.

As her fingers moved nimbly to adjust my postulant veil, I looked up at the smooth hands and recalled how, at thirteen, while I was a boarder at the academy, I'd taken in every detail about Sister Rosalie.

On warm Saturday afternoons when it was her turn for supervised recreation, we boarders went outside to the garden "summerhouse"—a pergola with cream-colored ionic columns and ivy-covered latticework. Sitting on a bench beside Sister Rosalie while some of the other girls played hopscotch or marbles, I watched her remove from her pocket a tiny scissors and thimble and a large white handkerchief. She busied herself poking the needle into the fabric of the handkerchief, stitching strands of red embroidery thread into little Xs that formed her identification number in the congregation: 1367 loomed larger in my brain than the dates of the Battle of Hastings or the Magna Carta.

Sister Rosalie sometimes put her sewing aside and pulled her fingers until the knuckles cracked, creating a popping sound. Some of the boarders were fascinated by the *pop* and would say, "Do it again, Sister." I hated it. The sound made me cringe. Sister Rosalie said that in her teen years, her mother had warned her that she would end with ugly fingers.

But there was nothing ugly about Sister Rosalie. Not even the enlarged knuckles detracted from her manicured hands. And the immaculate white frame encircling her face accented her brown eyes and olive complexion. She looked (borrowing one of my mother's expressions) as if she had "just stepped out of a bandbox."

I'd been attracted to Sister Rosalie from my first days at the Sacred Hearts Academy, where I'd spent a year as an eighth-grade student. It was she who'd noticed me first and invited me to assist with tidying up her classroom after school. Each day, at the sound of the dismissal bell, I packed up my books and leaped up the mahogany staircase to her room on the third floor of the old mansion that housed the elementary school.

I dusted the moveable oak desks, checked spelling quizzes, and cut out bulletin board letters. Some days her sixth-grade students would be there, writing punishments or making up homework. After they left she would talk to me and ask questions. "What are you thinking about now?" she would ask.

"I don't know, Sister,"

Then I'd take a deep breath and sigh.

"What's that sigh for?"

"I don't know, Sister."

When we were alone in the classroom, she combed my hair, and I drank in the sensuousness of her touch on my scalp. I was so mesmerized by her voice that often I did not hear what she said, though I recall that sometimes she talked about her mother. Once she told me that her mother had seamed seventeen pieces of fabric together to make her a blouse. "Mothers make so many sacrifices," she said. "Your mother makes sacrifices, too."

"Mm," I said.

And I thought, that'd be the day that my mother would sew seventeen scraps together to make me *anything*. I'd never, in my life, seen my mother sew on a button. When I outgrew my dresses it was Grandma who came to let down the hems and put on the facing. Anyway, I didn't want to talk about my mother. It occurred to me that Sister Rosalie might be leading me, wanting me to open up. But my relationship with my mother was a secret that I didn't share with anyone—not even Sister Rosalie. Whenever the subject turned to mothers, I said nothing. I wondered if my silence said more than words.

Sister Rosalie awakened emotional stirrings in me such as I'd never experienced before. When she kissed me on the forehead, that kiss melted my insides. Yet, she belonged to God, and, although I *loved* her, I expressed my affection for her in ways that were somewhat akin to a knight protecting his lady. I'd rush out every morning from the boarders' dining room and wait for her at the cloister door. I felt privileged to carry her book bag and to accompany her on the three-block walk to the little academy.

Now, after five years I was back in this same convent, not as a boarder, but as an aspirant to religious life. In the small vesting room off the cloister corridor, I paid scant attention to the other candidates as they gathered around the center table waiting to be swathed in black. My focus was on Sister Rosalie as she dressed me in the postulant habit. My feelings for her remained, yet they were filtered through my consciousness of the boundaries of religious life.

The child in me longed to recapture the halcyon days of boarding school. I had come back here to the Sacred Hearts Convent to live among the sisters as one of them.

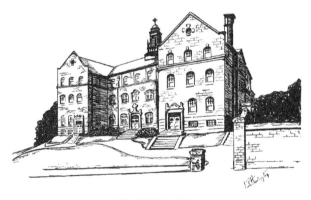

CONVENT 1936

The yellow cord suit and white pumps that I'd worn that morning had been whisked away by one of the nuns and deposited, I suppose, into a storage bin. Now black cotton hose and lace-up granny oxfords replaced my worldly clothes, and my red lipstick had been scrubbed off. A long-sleeved woolen dress and cape covered every inch of my body except my face and hands. Over the dress a black serge apron was double-tied around my waist. The only relief from black was the linen collar on my neck and a thin strip of white piping under my veil.

Suddenly nothing seemed real. I was Alice in the rabbit hole, growing nine feet tall. There were no mirrors in the dressing room, but when I looked down at the long dress, my height seemed disproportionately tall and my figure had disappeared under layers of dark wool.

Sister Rosalie stood on tiptoe to toss the crucifix's silken cord over my veil. Then she stepped back to assess my look. With a wink, she pushed a straggling curl out of the way. "Marion, I don't know how you'll manage to keep your hair from showing," she said.

When our group of nine was ready, we assembled in the corridor according to rank. Earlier, the sister-portress had noted our arrival time and registered our names in the convent archives. First arrivals were accorded higher seniority and they settled into their places at the rear of the line. The *youngest* went to the front.

In single file we moved along the cloister corridor

where cones of light filtered in through the purple-tinted windows. Rounding the corner we passed into the chapel and were directed to our places in the rear pews behind the black forms of kneeling sisters. The gothic chapel, resembling a small church, was not new to me, since I'd gone to daily Mass there as a boarder. I remembered the white marble altar and the mural depicting the Transfiguration. I saw the De Prato statues of Blessed Mother and St. Joseph and the carved walnut altar railing where we took communion. I recalled the high stained-glass windows and the fourteen ceramic Stations of the Cross. It was a nostalgic experience, putting me in mind of hearing the nuns chanting the Office on dark winter mornings as we boarders, still half asleep, made our way up the aisle for prayers before Mass.

Now, as I knelt in place, I observed a sister with a long taper, lighting the beeswax candles in the slanted brass candelabras. Calla lilies and white roses adorned the altar. There was an air of expectancy, and, except for a few coughing noises, the only sounds were from the muted organ chords as Sister Clare Adrienne played the soft strains of a Bach fugue. I knew it had to be Sister Clare Adrienne because, despite her infirmity, she was the most talented organist in the convent. I'd often been drawn to the chapel, as a boarder, when I heard her playing trills on the organ, and I'd wondered how she was able to do the footwork. The polio she'd contracted as a child had left her with partial paralysis in one leg.

I reflected on the first time I'd observed her walking unevenly around the circular courtyard, reading her psalm book. She stepped forward in her elevated shoe and drew the good leg out in a way that slowed her gait. From my perspective as a dreamy pre- adolescent, there was something romantic about the lame, black-veiled figure limping around the circle—like Jennifer Jones in the 1943 movie *The Song of Bernadette*.

A burst of notes from the upper register signaled the beginning of the ceremony. We neophyte postulants watched as those who'd completed their year of candidacy marched up the aisle, each holding aloft a lighted candle. The soon-to-be novices walked solemnly, stopping about midway in the nave. They genuflected in unison and rose again. They ascended the steps to the sanctuary, their gauze-like outer veils drawn over their faces. They bowed toward the bishop, who waited on the altar step to receive their promises, and knelt before him.

"My daughters, what do you ask?" he began.

"Your Excellency, it is with humility that we ask to be admitted into the Congregation," they answered in chorus and bowed as they read from their black-bordered cards.

"And is it of your own free will that you make this request?"

"It is, Your Excellency, and we pray that God may accept our sacrifice and perfect it in His mercy."

"Do you renounce Satan?"

"We do, Your Excellency."

"And all his works?"

"We do renounce them."

The strong perfume of lilies, the smoky waves of incense in the sanctuary, the organ and the chorus of voices cast a spell on me. I heard no more words. I watched the scene as if suspended in space.

The postulants rose from their knees and bowed to the bishop. As a sister handed each of them the folded and newly blessed habits they were to wear, they stepped down from the sanctuary. Eyes cast down, they exited the chapel and crossed the corridor to the community room where they would be clothed like medieval nuns. The bishop intoned the Ve-*ni, Cre-e-a-to-or, Spi-ri-tus*. Then the voices of a hundred sisters carried the Gregorian strains of the hymn that rose to the rafters as one single voice.

Minutes later I watched the now-transformed postulants enter the chapel as newly clothed novices. The only distinguishing feature between them and the professed sisters was the newness of their look in the starched bands that framed their faces. Under the weight of the merino shawls and heavy serge dresses, they moved more slowly than before. They looked like saints, their rosy cheeks highlighted by the reflected light of the burning candles that they held aloft.

I was transfixed by the music, the choir of nuns' voices, and the solemnity of the ritual as the novices ascended the steps inside the sanctuary. After the bishop pronounced the religious names that they would assume in the Congregation, the novices, in turn, approached the provincial superior and bowed profoundly.

The ceremony concluded with the singing of the *Te Deum*. Finally the organ intoned the recessional march and the novices filed out of the chapel, followed by the community of nuns. We new postulants took our places at the end of the line and, as we crossed the threshold, I heard happy refrains of "Congratulations, Sister." A blur of black-and-white forms lined the cloister corridor and the sisters were hugging, their starched white bands making a crunching sound as they brushed against one another.

The nuns exuded warmth, and I remembered how, as a boarder, I'd been impressed by their joyous spirit. I was happy to be joining such a vibrant community of women. They received me now with the convent embrace. "Welcome, Marion." Sister Marie Denise had to stretch and reach up her arms to hug me. Everything about her was diminutive, even her teeth. Then I noticed a plump older sister, her veil askew, talking to one of the newly professed. It was Sister Mary Aloysia, the *baseball nun*. Since my days as a boarder, Sister Mary Aloysia was freeze-framed on a garden bench with her portable radio, listening to the Red Sox. I'd thought it curious that a nun would be interested in baseball, but soon I learned not to disturb her when she was tuned in to Fenway Park. Once when I approached her and said, "Good afternoon, Sister," she waved me away with a dismissive gesture and leaned in closer to hear the score. It must have nearly killed her when the chapel bell rang in the middle of a game— especially when the Red Sox were down 3-0 in the ninth and Ted Williams belted one out of the park. It amused me to think that a nun could be so human. I knew nothing then about baseball, but that was the year the Red Sox won their sixth American League Championship. So no wonder Sister Mary Aloysia was annoyed when I distracted her attention from the game.

Sister Rosalie stood by my side and reminded some of the older sisters that here was a former boarder now entering the Order. She seemed proud to introduce me as her protégé. The loud clanging of the bells for the noon Angelus put an end to chatter. We dropped to our knees and recited the antiphoned Hail Marys until the bells peeled again, calling us to dinner.

All of the sisters were standing in place beside their chairs as we postulants trailed into the dining room and were directed to the last table near the windows. About eighty nuns and more than twenty novices, their heads lowered, faced the crucifix on the back wall. I strained to see Sister Rosalie, but while I was looking around, a voice intoned: "*In the name of the Father…*" In chorus, we recited, "Bless us, O Lord and these Thy gifts…" At the *Amen* there was a noisy scuffing of chairs as everyone sat down.

Tiny gifts tied up with ribbons were stacked beside the

novices' place settings, and twisted crepe paper stream-ers had been looped across the room. White tablecloths covered the long, rectangular tables, giving them a ban-quet appearance. Dishes of fruit cocktail had been set at each place. Senior novices in blue work aprons wheeled in stainless steel carts bearing platters of sliced turkey and dishes of mashed potatoes and green beans.

Glancing up I caught sight of Sister Rosalie at the farthest table. The noise rose to a high level as the nov-ices and all the sisters talked excitedly. Some older nuns craned their necks to see the former postulants in their new habits.

At our table we were getting acquainted with our com-panions. Mary Hildegarde from Baltimore looked like the all-American girl. Yvette, the tough-looking postulant from Woonsocket, talked out of the side of her mouth. Jenny had entered once before and then left after three weeks. She'd begged to come back, but had to wait a year before they would accept her. Second time around, she had an insider's knowledge. "Don't expect to be talking at meals after today," she said.

"What, Jenny, what did you say?"

"Just that silence is the rule here. You'll be able to talk at Christmas, New Year's, and a few saints' days."

I relegated Jenny's information to a corner of my mind. Part of my attraction to the sisters was the friendly way they'd interacted with each other during my year at the academy. They'd not only talked—they'd laughed, they'd seemed happy. I didn't want to believe Jenny. Maybe she didn't know what she was talking about.

One after another, we put our spoons down on our dessert plates and the room quieted in anticipation of the closing Grace. At the sound of the table bell, voices hushed. We rose to our feet, pushed our chairs in, and stood facing the crucifix. The Sligo lilt of Reverend Mother's voice punctuated the silence: "*In the nay-em of the Father...*" We joined in the prayer of thanks for the meal, and after the *Amen,* the room echoed with merriment as the sisters spilled out into the corridors to continue the celebration.

In the meantime our parents, excluded from the ceremony, had been waiting for us in the garden. It seemed unfair that they'd been served lunch in the high school dining room while we'd had our repast in the refectory. But nuns could not eat in front of seculars, and our parents were seculars.

Now my parents and my two brothers would have their first look at my transformed self. I paused in the doorway—then advanced toward them. My mother, in dark glasses, was seated on a bench near the grotto. I wondered if she was shielding her eyes from the afternoon sun or whether she was masking the effects of too much late night drinking.

My father, usually buoyant, stared at the ground, puffing smoke. Our eyes met and he reached down to stamp out his cigarette on the path.

Clothed in my black uniform, I was a mollusk in a shell—impervious to my own feelings and to the feelings of my parents. I stood before them, caressing the soft folds of my new garments and fingering the crucifix that hung from the cord around my neck. The color of mourning must have signaled death to them.

Marion with friend Irene

Silence hung heavy. Our last moments together were filled with the words we couldn't say. A loud clanging bell signaled the end of visiting hour. We moved slowly across the grounds to say our good-byes. The walls of the cloister had closed around us.

CONVENT 1886

The Initiation

After the last visitors had departed, Jenny and I took a stroll in the rose garden. The late afternoon light cast shadows on the gravel path as we rounded the corner by the statue of the Sacred Heart. I liked Jenny's humor and I wanted her to be my special friend.

We were relaxing in front of the summerhouse when suddenly we realized the novices and postulants must have gone inside. We quickened our steps and as we approached the novitiate porch, we saw a bent figure picking cigarette butts off the cobblestones It was Yvette   her veil hanging off the back of her head and her cape askew. The frazzled end of a cigarette hung from her lips as she gnawed the remains.

"Hey, got a match?" she asked.

"Those days are over, kiddo," Jenny said.

"Gee whiz! I need a smoke. I'm dyin'."

I looked hard at Yvette. *This girl isn't going to make it*, I thought. *I'll give her two weeks!*

"Better throw that thing away," Jenny said. "We have to go in now."

"Yeah, I know." Yvette yanked the nicotine stub out of her mouth and tossed it into some bushes near the music building.

The three of us approached the porch of the novitiate quarters. Novices and postulants were milling about in the corridor when we opened the door and stepped inside.

The novices seemed giddy. I looked at the friendly young faces framed in crinkly white bands and black veils. *They're so beautiful*, I thought. My heart did a leap to see Mary Maguire's winsome Irish face peering out from her starched band. A novice she was, but still the same old Mary Maguire.

"Marion!" Her voice was ecstatic. She gave me a welcoming hug and, gesturing to the other novices, announced, "We were boarders together."

What I remembered most about Mary Maguire were her comedic antics and the pranks she pulled on the other boarders and, sometimes, on the nuns. Mary came from a large family in New York and she had a heart bigger than the Empire State Building.

Soon we were spinning in different directions as the most senior novices escorted us around, showing us the dormitories. We made our way along a narrow corridor where I noticed several rooms with curtained cubicles.

Jenny was abreast of me, and before I knew what was happening, she pulled me inside a tiny room with two cots. "We're taking this one!" she announced.

I studied the curious shape of the room with its spiral staircase leading to the bell tower. "I love it," I said.

No one seemed to be in charge, and apparently we were free to make our own decisions concerning dormitories. Later I would learn that this liberty was not the norm but the result of the novice mistress' transition. She was busy readying herself for her new position as councilor to the Mother General in France.

We left the dormitories and went in search of our trunks. There in the cellar we unpacked nightclothes and towels and took them to our room. For the rest of the day, we talked to the other postulants and explored our new surroundings.

The dull donging of a bell interrupted our meanderings. Suddenly, in the wake of the bell, there was silence. The novices lined up in the corridor and we postulants followed them into a classroom furnished with student desks.

"We're here for *instruction time*," Mary whispered. She guided me to a seat in the front of the room. "Every day at five o'clock."

Seconds later everyone rose as Mother Winifred Marie, the novice mistress, strode into the room and walked briskly to the teacher's desk. It was my first chance to get a good look at her—a small-framed woman who appeared to be around sixty years or so. Most remarkable was her smile, at once reassuring.

"Good afternoon, Mother," everyone chorused.

Mother nodded. "Please be seated," she said, sliding into her chair. Her broad smile revealed a gold filling in one of her front teeth. I liked the way she looked directly at us and said, " Welcome to the new postulants."

"Poor things! No one has paid much attention to you today. We're in a state of flux here. You've probably heard that I'll be leaving in two weeks."

Groans from the novices. "Now, now," she went on, "in religious life we must accept God's will. Until I leave I'll be available to you for whatever you need. If I'm not in my office, you can probably catch me in the cellar, where I'll be packing my trunk."

"Oh, Mother!" someone wailed from behind.

Mother ignored the outburst and went on. "Tonight's instruction is on the vow of poverty. There is the *vow* of poverty, but more important, the *spirit* of poverty. When you understand that, you will become detached from material things and live in communion with God.

"Nothing belongs to us. Everything is held in common. Our Holy Rule says, 'They will husband with care all community property and see that it is maintained in order.' Those are the words of our founder, Father Debrabant.

"If you break something you must report it to your

superior. You drop a cup and it breaks—you take the cup to your superior and you say, 'Mother, I broke this cup.' Then your superior may or may not give you a penance."

"Yeah," interrupted Yvette, "but what if it was cracked or somethin'?"

"We don't offer any excuses," said Mother.

"Yeah, I know that, but what if it wasn't yer fault?"

Mother smiled, suppressing a laugh. Behind me someone giggled.

I was thinking, *Wow! That Yvette! Doesn't she get it? At this rate she'll be lucky to get through* one *week.*

After the evening instruction we lined up, stopping in the hallway to retrieve our prayer books from our assigned cubbyholes. We were on the march again, silently traversing the stairs and the long cloister corridor that connected the novitiate with the main convent. At the threshold of the chapel, we lowered our outer veils, covering our faces, waiting for the signal to enter. Through the thin gauze of the chapel-veil, I could make out the silhouette shapes of the professed nuns kneeling there in silence.

Crack! There was no mistaking the sound of the clapper. Two by two we moved forward like a garrison and processed up the aisle.

Another brisk sound of the clapper and we were on our knees, genuflecting together. Everybody down. Then up. Slipping silently into pews.

Then as a clear voice intoned a Latin psalm, we were on our feet. The plain chant, sung like voices of boy sopranos, echoed back, swelling at the beginning of each phrase and muting the last syllables to a pianissimo. Voices from both sides of the chapel rose as one in undulating rhythm. Taking our cues from the novices, we postulants followed the rubrics—standing at the intonation of a new psalm, alternately sitting, rising again, and bowing for each *Gloria Patri*. Holding my new office book in both hands, I followed the Latin and joined my voice to those of my sisters. I was no longer a boarder. I was one of them.

In the refectory we ate a simple meal—cold cuts of bologna and salami with sliced white bread. For dessert— prune plums in sweet syrup. Enamel pitchers, filled with cocoa, were passed hand-to-hand down the long refectory table.

All of the postulants seemed more somber now. There was little talking among us. However much the anticipation of this new life might have been fraught with uncertainties, now we were inside. Was it going to be everything we'd thought it would be? We were about to find out.

The Awakening

"Hey! Rise and shine! Time to get up, sleepy head."

"Wha...what?"

Jenny was shaking me out of my torpor. It couldn't be morning already, I thought. It felt like the middle of the night.

"I can't believe you slept through the bell—it's right over our heads!"

I rolled over on the narrow cot and yawned. "Get up now," Jenny said. "You're going to be late for chapel."

"Oh," I groaned. Jenny, already dressed, was making her bed.

I dragged myself off the thin mattress and headed for the bathroom. On my way back to the dorm, I heard the ringing of a little hand bell—the signal to line up. Like bees coming out of a hive, the novices and postulants poured out of their rooms and got into formation. They moved down the stairs like a battalion in Napoleon's army. I'd have to go alone to the chapel and face the humiliation of being late on the first day.

I splashed cold water on my face from the enamel basin on the nightstand and did a cursory brushing of my teeth. I dressed quickly, stepping into my postulant dress and fastening the stiff linen collar around my neck. The cape hooked, I slid the crucifix cord over my head and put on the *old lady* Oxfords. Clutching the veil, I decided to put it on in transit. I tore down the stairs as fast as I could in the Cuban-heeled shoes, and slowed my pace as I neared the cloister corridor on the second floor.

The stillness of that dark, narrow passage conveyed a sense of the medieval, and I half expected to see a ghost. When I reached the end of the corridor, I turned left to the chapel entrance. Tiptoeing to the threshold I lingered there a moment, taking in the sea of silent black shapes. I turned to the holy water font and dipped my fingers in. Touching the water to my forehead, I blessed myself and stepped inside.

Quiet as a cat I began my solitary walk down the long aisle to the front pew. I crept along the seemingly endless expanse of the nave, genuflected, and crawled over two postulants to my assigned place.

The chapel was as quiet as the Mausoleum of Caria, and such silence amplified even the creaking of a floorboard. Burning candlewicks reverberated as they popped inside votive glasses on side altars. Everyone was sitting.

The clerestory window above our bench was open a crack, and cool air wafted in. Behind me someone took a coughing fit, and then more coughing sounds echoed all around. I blinked my eyes and tried to stay awake. My head began to bob, and despite all my efforts, I fell asleep. After a few minutes I woke up, corrected my posture, and tried to pray. My mind wandered hopelessly. Then, just as I thought the exercise would never end, a voice somewhere read an invocation. There was a loud rustling as everyone moved onto kneelers. A few more minutes of silence and then the chanting began.

One of the nuns intoned a Latin antiphon. We were on our feet, bowing at the *Gloria Patris*. I found the place in my book and joined my voice to the others.

Out of the corner of my eye, I watched a tall nun ascend the altar steps carrying a lighted taper to ignite the candles. We would have Mass. A few minutes later a grayhaired priest, dressed in a green chasuble, entered the sanctuary and bowed before the tabernacle. In a voice barely audible, he recited the opening prayer, *Introibo ad altare Dei*—I will go unto the altar of God.

He ascended the steps to the altar with his back to us. At intervals he turned to the congregation with his arms outstretched, his eyes cast down, and mumbled the Latin words.

There was something mysterious about the rubrics of the Mass, with its ritualistic gestures and the priest's sotto voce Latin, the alternate standing, kneeling, sitting. The Offertory, when the priest raised the golden ciborium and we all bowed our heads in homage of the transubstantiation (which, according to Catholic doctrine, is the changing of bread and wine into Christ's body and blood).

At Communion Reverend Mother led the procession of nuns. They knelt at the wooden railing and tipped their heads back to receive the Hosts on their tongues. The priest held the chalice of white wafers aloft, pausing in front of each sister. *"Corpus Domine Jesu Christi."*

Returning to our places we bowed our heads and made our thanksgiving. The chapel was still and dark. Only the flames of vigil candles licking the glass and the softly murmured words of the priest: "Ite Missa est." The Mass was finished.

The sweet aroma of freshly brewed coffee wafted up from the kitchen below as we made our way along the corridor. All of the nuns were standing, facing the crucifix, when we entered the dining room. Their hands were folded in Gothic position as they waited to begin the *Prayer Before Meals*. Most had their eyes cast down, and only a few of the curious looked in our direction. No sooner had we chorused *Amen* than all the chairs were pulled out from the tables, creating a jarring sound as they scraped the hardwood floor.

No one spoke. Gone were the crepe paper streamers that had heralded the celebration of yesterday's feast. Dull oilcloth replaced the table linens, and the earthenware dishes looked poor and miserable. I watched the nuns unfurl their rolled-up napkins and fasten them to their habits with glass-headed pins. The novice-servers, in blue seersucker aprons, wheeled in steel carts laden with breakfast foods.

A nun went to a lectern in the center of the room. She opened a small book on the stand and read aloud:

"*The Imitation of Christ,* Chapter Seven, On Avoiding Vain Hope and Pride: Do not pride yourself because of your physical nature or your beauty, which may be marred by a small illness. Do not take pleasure in your natural gifts or your readiness of wit, lest you offend God, who created all the good whatever that you have received by nature. If there is any good in you, you should believe that there is much more in others, and so preserve your humility."

A server handed a bowl of fresh fruit to Mother Winifred. Plucking an orange out of the dish, Mother Winifred passed the bowl to Elizabeth, the solemn-faced postulant. I chose a shiny apple and cut it into quarters. The professed sisters and novices did not look around and seemed to have a silent mode of communication when they needed something. Elizabeth, also, kept her eyes down. *Wow*, I thought. *She seems oblivious to all this.* I wondered what everyone was thinking about. The reading selection made me feel melancholy. I thought of my school days here when all the nuns seemed so happy. I hadn't pictured it like this.

The reader went on: "All is vanity except to love God…"

Cereal was passed in serving bowls. I spooned some cornflakes into my dish and waited for the enamel milk pitcher to come down the line. The absence of talking accentuated the scrunch of metal spoons against the chunky earthenware, but at least those sounds lessened the tension of complete silence.

The Regimentation

Scant daylight peeked through the narrow cellar windows of the Prospect Street convent, casting shadows on the nuns' trunks, lined up in rows. Low-wattage lightbulbs hanging from the ceiling revealed soapstone sinks and padded ironing tables. Yvette and I had been sent to assist in the laundry. The space resembled a miniature factory—three or four novices ironing the starched guimpes, others folding clothes, and one, feeding wet laundry through the rotund washtub wringer. No one spoke. It was as if we were watching a silent movie.

At the end of the room that faced the garden, the bulkhead doors were folded back, ushering in the sunlight of a sultry August morning. Wicker laundry baskets of wet sheets were lined up near the steps, ready to be hung outside. The tall, thin novice, Sister Noreen Mary, gestured us toward the baskets and pantomimed our task.

I took hold of one basket handle and Yvette, the other.

With our skirts pinned back, we scaled the three steps of the bulkhead and skipped into the green-latticed enclosure reserved for hanging laundry. We set the basket on the ground and pulled out the first sheet. Stretching it out, we squared the corners and pegged it to the line. After we'd hung several more sheets, I picked up the empty basket and was on my way back to the cellar when Yvette sighed and leaned against a fence post.

"What's the matter," I asked.

"Gee whiz," she said, "I wish I had a cigarette now."

I didn't know what to say. Not being a smoker, I had no idea about nicotine withdrawal. It must have been very hard for her to stop cold, but she was determined. "C'mon," she said. "Let's go in."

It had been a relief to go outside and get a breath of fresh air, even though the sun was sweltering. Porting the willow basket on my right hip and descending the bulkhead steps, I paused to get my bearings. The contrast of the bright light in the yard and the darkness inside was an adjustment for the eyes.

The novices were still standing at the tables, clamping the irons down on the guimpes to stiffen the collars. Sister Noreen Mary hefted a heavy antique iron from the stove and set it on a metal stand while she prepared her guimpes for ironing. I was glad to see that the other novices had joined the twentieth century and were using electric models.

A distance away from the laundry space, Sister Mary Declan stood over a galvanized tub of brownish liquid, stirring it with an old broom handle. She churned the mixture of lye and fat as if she were making butter instead of laundry soap. In the corner two novices sat at a small gas-propelled apparatus, feeding starched wet strips of cotton batiste into a ridged, revolving turbine that cooked them into the crinkly cookie bands they wore around their faces.

Only my third day here and already the regimentation was suffocating. How, I thought, would I ever get used to this silence?

Rule Number One: They will speak only when necessary.

But couldn't I tell a joke if I wanted to? And the going back and forth from the chapel to the refectory, the refectory to the chapel, down that long corridor. I saw myself in an endless procession of black-clad forms moving silently through the halls. How would I endure this for my whole life?

Sister Noreen Mary had her Holy Rule open on the ironing table. I watched her as she took up a wet guimpe, dripping with starch. She rubbed the material to create a kind of friction before laying it down on the padded table. Waiting for the iron to heat, she bent slightly and I could see that she was reading the Rule to herself.

On the previous day in the cellar, a couple of novices

had read articles of the Rule aloud. There in the otherwise silent and semi-dark atmosphere of the cellar, they read:

ARTICLE 50: "They will keep silence, speaking only for necessity, that they may remain in communion with God."

ARTICLE 51: "They will…"

I was blanking out. Most of the articles that I heard seemed to start with: "They will not" or "They shall not."

In their fervor, I supposed the novices were trying to emulate the saints. But I was overwhelmed by the austerity. I wondered if this was the right place for me.

Yvette and I finished hanging the clothes and returned to do more cellar work. My next assignment was ironing the community handkerchiefs. I reached for one of the modern irons and plugged it in. After the handkerchiefs were ironed, they were folded in half and then half again so they ended up in little squares. The task was repetitive, but somehow soothing. I was lost in my reverie.

Suddenly Sister Noreen Mary's voice broke the silence. "Sacred Heart of Jesus," she prayed.

A chorus of novices responded, "Have mercy on us."

"Sacred Heart of Jesus."

"Have mercy on us."

On and on it went—this litany. I remained mute. I was prayered out. This was worse than silence. I stood up and went to the ironing table. "Why do you have to pray out loud?" I said. "Isn't it enough that we pray all day in the chapel? All we do around here is eat and pray, EAT AND PRAY."

I sat down. The novices kept their composure. But somewhere behind me I heard a muffled giggle. I turned and saw Mother Winifred Marie crouched behind her trunk, holding her sides and doing her best not to laugh out loud.

The Move to Rock Street

Today was moving day! Furnishings from the old novitiate building had been delivered to our new quarters in a recently acquired house on Rock Street, about three blocks away from the Prospect Street Convent. The move was necessary for the Order to be in compliance with the norms of Canon Law, which proscribed novices from mixing with the professed religious except for chapel and refectory.

The transition was not easy for the senior novices, who had spent the major part of their novitiate here at the motherhouse, and for those of us who had entered only three weeks before, it was an adjustment. In addition, we had heard rumors that the new novice mistress was very strict.

After breakfast, bidding teary farewells to Mother Winifred, we spilled out into the courtyard and waited for the last stragglers. Only the second week in September, and already there was a sense of autumn in the air. A cool north wind blew across the yard from the music building to the cul-de-sac outside the cloister corridor. The sky was pure azure without a trace of cloud, and sunlight glinted off the leaves of the chestnut tree. Silently we glided into place, our black forms wrapped in knitted shawls to ward off the morning chill. The only audible sounds, except for a few birds chirping, were of thin leather soles tapping the cobblestones as we assembled. Postulants in front of novices, we arranged ourselves in twos and waited.

We'd been told that the new novice mistress would not arrive for another two weeks, and a newly appointed assistant novice mistress would be temporarily in charge.

This was Sister Therese Gertrude, and the minute I saw her I recognized that she had been the convent portress when I was a boarder. Sister Therese Gertrude was as thin as a spindle. Instead of a clapper she signaled us to move along by a throaty *"Ahem."*

Walking double file, our heads inclined, hands concealed in sleeves, we passed through the iron gateway and stepped into the road. I turned and stole a last look at the beloved convent that held many memories for me of boarding school.

We moved along as purposefully as a colony of ants. Now and then a man or a woman passed by, but we did not look up to meet their gaze. We crossed another street until we were parallel with the fire station, and then descended the hill toward the river. We were in a different neighborhood with larger houses and wider lawns. We stopped in front of a white Victorian set back from the street. The yard was circumscribed by a driveway of crushed stone, and the overhanging branches of a massive copper beech tree dominated the landscape.

We approached the house from the side entrance, which opened into a kitchen with cream-colored wainscoting and matching cabinets. A table and some chairs had been placed near the window, and patterned green linoleum covered the floor.

We crossed a hallway to a small sewing room with dark paneled walls and built-in storage cupboards. The room was pleasant, with light coming in from one large window. Two Singer treadle machines stood waiting to stitch our black clothes.

Next we entered a long, narrow room with a fireplace. It must have been the family dining room when the former owners lived there, but now it was furnished with a long pine table and eight bentwood chairs. The flooring was hardwood, although a worn oriental carpet covered most of the area. This would be our community room, and it connected to another room with a large bay window, facing the side street. Shiny, shellacked school desks—the old-fashioned kind with wrought-iron frames, designed to be bolted to the floor—were freestanding in rows of threes. A larger desk took up the alcove space in front of the bay window, and I assumed it was for the new novice mistress.

Off the classroom, to the left, French doors opened

onto a solarium that gave a view of the gardens where roses still bloomed. Built-in bookshelves housed neat volumes of literature and poetry. A long settee in front of the wall of windows beckoned me to revisit this sanctuary.

A center hall staircase with a mahogany balustrade led upstairs. On the second floor each of five bedrooms had been divided into four cubicles. White opaque curtains, drawn back along ceiling rods, revealed narrow beds covered with white cotton seersucker or damask spreads. Beside each bed a small wooden nightstand held an enamel washbasin.

On the third floor—the former servants' quarters—more rooms held the same kinds of furnishings, but the rooms were smaller, with narrower windows. In the absence of anyone in authority assigning places, Norajean and I chose a room under the eaves with a sloped ceiling and thirties-vintage wall sconces. The fixtures held forty-watt bulbs, and a single dormer window let in light and gave a view of the street below. Two beds had been made up with cotton plissé coverlets, and although the room was narrow, it seemed more spacious because it was not curtained off.

In the dormitory adjacent to ours, while some novices were quietly organizing their wardrobes, Norajean and I giggled and talked, relieved to have a day without structure. We went to the cellar and brought back treasured things from our trunks.

I remember our first night there. Norajean had a box of licorice that her aunt had sent her. We lay on our beds long after the curfew, sucking on the pastel coated candies, talking and giggling, and ignoring the Grand Silence. Suddenly the door opened a crack, and a ghostly, white lace-trimmed sleeve reached up and pulled the chain on our wall light.

It was Sister Therese Gertrude.

The Rock Street property extended back a city block. A high stone wall—monastic-looking—enclosed the acreage along the side street and joined at right angles with the wall behind the grape arbor on the lowest terrace. The grape arbor was really a pergola with a graveled space underneath for walking. In the center of the garden path was a small round gardener's shed that resembled a dollhouse. The door to it was partially open, revealing some cobwebs on the windows and a few rusty tools.

The morning after our arrival, some of us hung out in the garden, helping ourselves to the grapes on the arbor. Suddenly the ringing of a small bell summoned us inside. We followed a group of novices into the community room, where the rest of the group was seated. What was happening? Reverend Mother Gabriel Clare, the provincial superior, was there waiting for us to get settled.

She looked at each one as if gathering us all to her bosom. Her eyes were as blue as cornflowers and she smiled before she spoke. "Welcome, Sisters," she said, and right away I knew by the lilt in her voice that she was Irish. I studied her face, its ruddy complexion.

What is it about her that is so beautiful? I wondered. Her face was too long and her teeth overlapped. Yet there was something captivating about her, something indefinable.

She was like a grandmother and probably the right age for that. I judged her to be about seventy. She was sorry, she said, that our Mother Mistress was not here at the beginning to welcome us. In the meantime Sister Therese Gertrude would see to our needs, and she, Reverend Mother, would come over from the adjoining building every day to see "how you are getting on, Sisters."

I could see by the mantel clock that it was almost noon, but Reverend Mother was ahead of me.

"And now, Sisters, 'tis nearly dinnertime and you must be hungry. Sure the sign of a true vocation is a healthy appetite."

Then standing she addressed Sister Therese Gertrude:

"Sister, I think we'll have talking at dinner today."

"Oh, thank you, Reverend Mother," we all chorused as we rose to our feet and shuffled into line to go to the refectory.

The Formation

Everything changed the day Mother Consolata came to be our novice mistress. For Norajean and me it was the end of leisurely walks in the garden, hanging out in the grape arbor, plucking the purple fruit off the vine, and consuming as many of the succulent grapes as we could stuff into our mouths. Since leaving the monastic regime at the Prospect Street Convent, we'd reveled in this semi-structured environment in our new quarters—lazing about in the terraced gardens, reading books pilfered from the library next door at the provincial house. Disregarding the rule of silence, we told each other stories of our lives, and spoke of what had drawn us to enter this Order of nuns.

Reverend Mother Gabriel Clare's office was in the provincial building—St. Helena's—and she rarely came to the novitiate. No one was in charge except Sister Therese Gertrude, whose sole concern, it seemed, was to instruct us in sewing. Sister Therese Gertrude knew nothing about novices and postulants or what to do with us, and we'd taken full advantage. We did go to chapel and refectory, but, in the absence of structure, we seized freedom and made our own rules. We could not know how this day would usher in a profound change in the order of things and affect our lives.

Norajean and I had been sitting on a cement wall in the lower garden, basking in the morning sun, when the loud clanging of a bell startled us.

We looked at each other, surprised to hear a bell at this hour. We swallowed the remains of our forbidden fruit, spitting out the seeds as we sprang across the terrace and scrambled inside. All the novices and postulants were already assembled in the community room. Everyone's eyes were on us as we slid into two vacant chairs. Reverend Mother Gabriel Clare was there, and a very tall nun stood beside her.

"Sisters," said Reverend Mother, "I want to introduce your new novice mistress, Mother Consolata. I hope you will emulate her." The way Reverend Mother said *emulate* was how she said all the words in her Irish way, like—imitate, appreciate, promulgate. Accenting the third syllable, it sounded like em/u/late.

As my eyes sized up our novice mistress (and there was a lot to size up because she looked about ten feet tall), I wondered if all the rumors we'd heard were true—that Mother Consolata was a "living rule," that she "ran a tight ship." Ascetic-looking, she was like a tall stalk of thin asparagus. As she greeted us with a smile, I was studying her face to fathom the depths of her personality. I knew this was a new assignment for her and that she'd been superior of the convent in New York before coming here. There wasn't much time for her to speak to us because after a few moments a bell rang for the noon exercise and we were off to chapel.

My first real impression of her came later in the day. We were seated by seniority in the classroom, everyone facing the executive desk in front of the bay window. Isolated in our thoughts, we waited for Mother Consolata to appear. The suspense was palpable, the normal silence notched up a degree or two. Waiting. Endless waiting.

Suddenly, like a bird flapping its wings, the skirts of her habit swooshed and the silhouette of Mother Consolata glided up the aisle to the front of the room. We were on our feet, chorusing, "Good evening, Mother."

Standing behind the swivel chair of the large oak desk, she acknowledged our greeting by a slight nod of her head and motioned us to sit down. She took her assumed place and sat straight up in her chair, as if supported by steel vertebrae.

Laying some notes in front of her, she began to speak and, at once, her mellifluous voice seduced me. I was hearing a running melody sprinkled with word fragments, but I was focused on her, not the message. She looked so perfect in the habit, as though she'd been born in it. The white starched band was a sort of halo around her face. The initial impression I'd formed of her from listening to gossip— all that was gone now. The timbre of her voice was enchanting me like a siren.

When I did pick up on the threads of the instruction, she was saying something about the calling, what it meant to have a vocation. We were called to a holy life, and by following the Rule we would be sanctified. "Whatever motivated you to enter religious life, the fact is you are here now. God has called you. Any doubts about your vocation you must put in the bosom of the Sacred Heart."

All the time Mother was speaking, I thought it strange that she did not make eye contact with anyone. We'd been told to bring our hand sewing to the instruction, and most of the time I was focused on making little hemming stitches on my name tags. My desk was in the front row, and when, occasionally, I glanced up, it seemed as if Mother were looking out like an actor from a stage, not really seeing us.

She continued, "During this time of trial in the novitiate, the devil may tempt you to give up your vocation. He doesn't want you to serve Our Lord. If you have any doubts about your vocation, you must come to me, not talk to each other. Postulants and novices do not have the grace to help you. And pray! Pray for perseverance, Sisters."

Not talk to each other! I was curious to know what the other postulants thought about that. Most of us were just out of high school. Were they, like me, surprised by this injunction, I wondered. Did they feel this was the life they'd expected? I wanted so much to talk to them, to hear how they were feeling. I glanced around, breaking yet another rule, but in their faces I saw that no one other than myself seemed nonplussed.

Finally the instruction was over. Mother Consolata's fingers reached for the small hand bell on her desk. She shook it gently and the bell tingled. God's voice was calling us. Out of deference, we waited for Mother to pass, and then we all queued up in ranking order for the chapel.

Maybe it was the next day or the day after that we were introduced to our schedule:

5:40	Rise, make bed
6:00	Line up to cross yard
6:05	Meditation in chapel
6:30	Canonical Hours: Prime, Terce, Sext, None (chanting of the Office)
7:00	Mass
7:30	Breakfast
7:50	Breakfast wash-up
8:00	Functions
8:30	Cellar: washing, ironing
10:00	Morning tea
10:15	Normal school; manual work; sewing of habits; miscellaneous projects

11:40	Examination of Conscience
12:00	Dinner
12:30	Recreation
1:30	Laundry: folding and distributing clean clothes
2:00	Reading of New Testament and other spiritual reading
3:00	Study and homework for classes
4:00	Afternoon tea
4:15	Vespers and rosary in chapel
5:00	Instructions
6:00	Matins and Lauds in chapel
6:30	Supper
7:00	Recreation
8:00	Night Prayers in chapel (Beginning of Grand Silence)
8:15	Dormitory: washing up
9:00	Lights out

Our sleeping quarters were changed. Norajean and I were moved out of our cozy attic alcove. We were split up and assigned new places in rooms with curtained cubicles—four or five postulants and novices to a room. There was just enough space in each cubicle for a single iron cot, a chair, and a nightstand. Speaking in the dormitories was expressly forbidden. If you made eye contact or spoke to anyone in the dormitory or the corridor after night prayers, it was a violation of the Grand Silence, and you were obliged to report the incident to Mother Consolata.

A list of work assignments, called *functions*, was tacked to the bulletin board in the community room. The chapel function was coveted by the novices who liked working in a holy place. The refectory was a heavy-duty job, requiring the moving of all the chairs and sweeping under the tables. Once a week all the place settings, salt and pepper shakers, and vinegar cruets had to be taken off the tables so the oilcloth could be scrubbed clean, waxed by hand, and buffed to a shine.

We swept hallways and corridors daily, dusted mopboards, cleaned bathrooms and parlors, brushed dirt from the staircases. Saturday was the day for big cleaning. We washed the wide-planked floors and applied Butcher's paste wax to the wood. We buffed the floors to a spit polish shine with an electric buffer and oiled the wainscoting and furniture with a special linseed mixture.

In addition to the regular functions, some novices were assigned to iron the cotton batiste bands that served as face framing underneath the veil. About two and a half inches wide, the bands were dipped into a bath of hot starch and left to dry; then plunged into a basin of cold liquid starch before being fed into the band machine (itself a relic from France). Working as a pair, one novice fed the band onto a grooved cylinder above the gas flame while her partner turned the crank. Sometimes walking past the utility room,

I smelled the heat generated from the little machine. And a few times, but rarely—there was an odor of scorch. Most of the time, the limp cloth emerged converted into a band of crisp white pleats resembling the fluted papers found in cookie tins. In the novitiate hierarchy "doing the bands" was a prestigious vocation within a vocation.

Novices were issued a change of bands once a week. Fragile and susceptible to humidity, the pleated bands had to be placed between two sheets of cardboard at night so they would retain their shape. The novices fastened the cardboard presses with rubber bands and stuck them under their mattresses before getting into bed.

Gradually we postulants assimilated the customs and learned how to care for our clothes. Every Saturday afternoon we changed into our Sunday habits and cleaned our weekday dresses and veils. Using a stiff brush we removed any stains with Lava soap. The novices spread out their long, rectangular shawls and cleaned them, in tandem, while maintaining custody of the eyes. Then they dampened them before folding them and putting them between boards.

This ritual was a carry-over from the nineteenth-century French nuns. Indeed it was de rigueur to put the separate parts of your habit in boards to press the creases. Some novices had very old wooden boards—hand-me-downs, I suppose, from some of the deceased sisters—while most of us new arrivals had pressboard or particleboard.

The boards were drawn tight with rope or cord and placed near the furnace to get the maximum heat for the creases. On Sunday night before retiring, we removed the weekday habits and put the Sunday ones in boards. Then we turned them in to the linen room. Failure to comply drew a reprimand from Mother Consolata.

Toward the end of September, we began our studies in the Normal School. Sister John Elizabeth (whom I'd known since my boarding-school days) taught English literature. An enthusiastic teacher, she introduced us to Beowulf and *The Canterbury Tales*. How I enjoyed Sir Gawain and the Green Knight and the poetry of John Donne. Analyzing poetry and picking out figures of speech delighted me. I loved the cadence and music of the poems. Going to class was a welcome respite from scrubbing floors.

Sister Adrienne Mary from our convent in Southampton, England, taught elocution. She made us memorize non-sense jingles for pronunciation like *la loo lie loo lilly loo lay* and recite them, drawing out the syllables in an exaggerated way. Yvette couldn't seem to master the "ING" sound. "Ah," Sister Adrienne would exclaim, directing her attention at Yvette—"RIDING, RIDING, the highway man came RIDING!"

By October the air had cooled. Mornings, at barely six o'clock, it was still dark outside and frost was in the air. We shivered in our shawls—the knitted woolen wraps that we wore around our shoulders. We shuffled our feet, side to side, waiting for the stragglers to line up so we could cross the yard to St. Helena's. I exhaled and my breath floated out like fog.

Then—the sound we'd been waiting for—the clap of wood on wood. At the signal our battalion moved forward over the gravel path, passing the storage barn and approaching the formidable gray building known as St. Helena's. We entered through the side door and deposited our wraps in the cloakroom. Moving noiselessly down the hallway, we stopped at the alcove under the staircase to retrieve our office books and missals from the assigned cubbyholes.

In formation again, like a fleet of swallows, waiting for the sound of the clapper. Forward march to the chapel. Up the aisle—soft shuffling of shoes. Listening for the cue. CLACK! Genuflection in unison. Rise. Enter pews. More shuffling of leather soles. Kneel down. Sit back. Try to stay awake.

After Mass we filed into the refectory, where the dominant feature of the room was a large veined marble fireplace. Above the mantel a beveled glass mirror reflected light from the windows opposite. Molded mahogany paneling divided the oyster-colored walls at the chair rail. The room's rectangular shape accommodated two long, wooden tables with enough bentwood chairs for forty sisters. Cream-colored oilcloth covered the tables, and heavy earthenware plates, bowls, cups, and saucers, along with water glasses, were set out at each sister's place. Everyone had a rolled-up napkin fastened with a long glass-headed pin.

Amidst these luxuriant accoutrements that had been installed by the original owner (probably a rich industrialist in the days of the Fall River textile mills), our own furnishings reflected monastic simplicity for the sisters, if not for the higher superiors.

At the two extreme ends of the room, double doors opened onto the corridor. The first double door was for Reverend Mother Gabriel and the second for the professed religious, novices and postulants, in that order. A smaller door in the rear of the refectory was reserved for the novice mistress.

Reverend Mother Gabriel Clare, as provincial superior, was accorded the head seat at the table of the professed sisters. In observance of Canon Law the novitiate shared, with the professed, only the chapel and the refectory.

Each week two novices or postulants were assigned to wait on tables. They left the chapel several minutes before the end of the spiritual exercises to set up the serving trays. Skirts pinned up, blue seersucker aprons tied around their waists, they moved quickly, handing dishes to the superiors, who passed them down the tables. The superiors were the only ones to have their tea or coffee poured for them— a mark of respect for the office. It was my impression that neither Mother Gabriel Clare nor Mother Consolata relished the attention, but accepted it as custom.

When Reverend Mother Constanza came from France for visitation, the propriety changed. Because of her rank as councilor to Mother General, she sat at the head of the Religious table with Mother Gabriel Clare to her right. Mother Constanza's place was set with a linen tablecloth and fine porcelain dishes. Her private server went into the corridor and entered ceremoniously through the double doors to pour her tea. In ballet-like movements the novice served Mother Constanza her breakfast of scrambled eggs, toast points, and orange slices.

Mother Constanza was a grande dame. At about sixty years of age, she was still beautiful. She spoke softly, almost in a whisper. I pictured her in the court of Louis XVI dressed in organza like Marie Antoinette and attended by a bevy of ladies-in-waiting. Perhaps that's how she saw herself.

When she needed or wanted something, she pressed the bell at her place or beckoned to the server, who stood in vigilance. Once Sister John Veronica, no doubt nervous, tripped and fell against the table, knocking over a pot of tea that spilled some of its contents onto Mother Constanza's lap. Sister Veronica dissolved into tears. "Oh, Reverend Mother, forgive me," she said.

Pulling up her skirt, Mother Constanza sprang from her chair. "Oh, my dear," she said, "don't worry. It's not like committing the least venial sin."

Mother Constanza came and went intermittently from

the Mother House in Rome, and we never knew when she was due for a visit. When she was in the house, it was her prerogative to chant the blessing during the evening Office. Normally the presiding novice would rise, face the back of the chapel, and intone the antiphon, bowing to Mother Gabriel Clare. All of us were accustomed to hearing Mother Gabriel's gravelly voice as she chanted the response.

On occasion we would be startled by hearing, instead, the operatic voice of Mother Constanza chanting the Latin words with the flourish of a diva. "Per virginem matrem concedat…" Suddenly on hearing this we convulsed in laughter and doubled over, unable to continue chanting the Holy Office. No sooner was there a pause than we began rollicking again so that the wooden benches seemed to vibrate.

Whether because of embarrassment or annoyance, our novice mistress signaled her disapproval of our breach of religious decorum. But her *tsk, tsk* only seemed to propel us into more gales of laughter. This unrestrained behavior would earn us a reprimand later, but, at the time, it was a release of pent-up tension.

When my parents came to visit after the allowed seven-week period, my father asked what I thought about the upcoming election (1952). I told him what Mother Consolata had said about Adlai Stevenson—that he was a communist. And to tell our parents not to vote for him.

"Heavens," said my mother, "Adlai Stevenson is a wonderful American."

"My God, don't you read the newspapers?" my father asked.

"No, Dad, it's Canon Law. Secular press is not allowed so that we can focus on our spiritual progress."

"Can't understand that!" he said. "Teaching order? How will you teach the children?"

I don't remember what I answered my father that day. In the brief interim between leaving home and living in the enclosed environment that was the novitiate, I'd left the me that I was behind and turned into another me.

In this cloistered environment without access to radio, newspapers, and magazines, we were cut off from our own culture and immersed in the culture of French nineteenth-century provincialism. The French superiors of the Congregation who came to Fall River to establish a boarding school for girls and young women had, themselves, been educated in conservative religious schools.

At seventeen or eighteen we were idealistic and impressionable, and we embraced our new life with zeal. We were unaware that much of what passed for normal in our confines was, in reality, very abnormal.

We learned about religious decorum and propriety. We were not to run on the stairs. When we walked we were not to swing our arms. Our hands were to be concealed under our capes. We had to walk as befit religious—holding ourselves erect without swinging the hips. To swing the hips was considered worldly.

We learned about custody of the eyes, keeping the eyes cast down, not looking around out of curiosity.

We learned about the value of silence. "Keep the rule of silence and the silence will keep you" was Mother Consolata's mantra.

On Sundays we did no manual work, and we ate grape-fruit, bacon and eggs, and sweet rolls. As Mass was coming to an end, the savory smell of cooked bacon wafted down the corridor and penetrated the closed oak doors of the chapel, producing an aroma so comforting that it was almost impossible to think of anything else. Sometimes I wondered if I were the only one who thought of food.

On Sunday mornings we did our spiritual reading, sitting at our desks while we waited turns for the weekly conference with Mother Consolata. It was quiet in the classroom, everyone reading the New Testament or *The Imitation of Christ*. From where I sat in the front row, I could hear the parlor door opening and closing. We went in order of seniority, and each postulant on exiting would gesture to the next in line.

I remember my first time— entering the room and closing the door behind me—Mother seated at a rectangular table. I stood before her. It went something like this:

"Good morning, Mother."

"Good morning, Sister"

"Do you have anything to tell me?"

"I don't think so, Mother."

"All right, Sister. You may enumerate your permissions."

"Thank you, Mother."

I read from the list I'd copied into my notebook:
"May I…"

drink water outside the refectory
use the supplies and tools necessary for my function
borrow and lend small articles
give and receive holy cards
speak when necessary
use pins and needles for my sewing

I hesitated. "Mother," I said, "I—I find it humiliating to ask for such little things."

"Yes, Sister. That's the idea. It keeps you humble."

On Sunday afternoons after recreation, we sat at our desks in the classroom. This was the time allotted for writing letters home to our parents, and the continuance of the weekly conference. Some novices and postulants were in and out of Mother's office in a matter of minutes, while others took longer.

Sister Albertine usually emerged from Mother's room with tears streaming from her eyes, her complexion all blotchy. I shouldn't have been looking, but it was hard not to notice, especially when she was blowing her nose and weeping. Sister Albertine seemed to be one of those novices who did everything correctly. She was one of the trusted ones to do the bands. I couldn't imagine Sister Albertine doing anything that would bring a reprimand, and I wondered what made her cry so.

Other novices and postulants, in turn, came out of the room, sat down, and resumed whatever they had been doing. Their faces betrayed no emotion. During this time we listened to classical music—always the same two 78s. Fritz Kreisler's "Schön Rosmarin" and Massenet's "Méditation" from *Thais*. Sister Helen William's parents had given the records to the novitiate along with a blonde wood phonograph console. Maybe there were other records in the collection, but these were the only two that Mother put on each Sunday. Not everyone appreciated the music, and Yvette, on more than one occasion, looked peeved when Mother Consolata approached the turntable. As soon as Mother had gone, Yvette would let out a sigh.

I looked forward to the Sunday afternoon concert. I would have enjoyed listening to the works of a wider variety of composers, but the plaintive tones of Kreisler and Massenet matched my melancholy mood. Sometimes when Mother didn't turn off the phonograph, the arm would automatically swing into position and Kreisler's bow would, again, begin the downstroke. From behind I'd hear Yvette clear her throat the way people do when they want to get your attention. I remember turning around once to face her. She pulled a face and rolled her eyes.

We remained seated at our desks most of the afternoon, reading the New Testament or *The Imitation of Christ*. Some of the novices used the time to make greeting cards to send home. Sister Albertine copied passages out of books in beautiful lettering. Apart from the obligation of the conference, this was the only unstructured time of the week. For me it was like a breath of fresh air.

At four o'clock the bell rang calling us to tea. We lined up in formation and went to the refectory in St. Helena's. We stood at our places and, facing the wall crucifix, we signed ourselves with the cross, touching our foreheads, breastbones, and shoulders. We said the Grace silently and sat down to tea. On Sundays, except during Advent and Lent, we usually found four or five chocolates in brown crinkly candy wrappers on our saucers. Because of our communal life we "handed in" the boxes of candy that our parents brought on visiting days, and usually the chocolates were distributed in this manner on Sundays and feast days. Sunday—a day without manual chores, time to think, to get blue. Chocolate drugged us.

On weekdays we had bread and jam or bread and molasses. Tea with milk was served in enamel pitchers that we passed to one another. Almost everyone hated the molasses, but I loved it because it reminded me of my grandmother making gingerbread. She'd always let me lick the molasses off the big spoon.

Mother Consolata insisted that everyone take at least one slice of bread after she discovered that some novices were dieting. Sister Bernadette Michael was under scrutiny for losing weight. In those days we didn't know about anorexia, but looking back I imagine that Sister Bernadette might have suffered from the disorder. Whether our novice mistress was aware I don't know, but I'd observed Sister Bernadette Michael stealing into the refectory and downing the contents of a vinegar cruet. She fainted in the chapel, as I remember, more than once. And then one day she disappeared. Sent home, most likely, for not having a true vocation.

For a while it seemed as if the place was getting decimated. Whenever you looked there was an empty place at the refectory table or the chapel. There was the novice, Sister Pauline, who seemed a little odd. She'd been assigned to assist the cook with meal preparation. Once when it was my turn to peel the potatoes, I observed Sister Pauline attempting to unmold some Jell-O from a tin. The operation didn't go well and the Jell-O plopped out into the soapstone sink next to some vegetable peelings.

"That's one for the postulants," she said.

Another time she baked two dozen oranges. Maybe

she'd had some idea for a gourmet dessert, but the oranges came out of the oven smashed and gooey. Seeing the mess she'd created, she threw a rolling pin across the table, just missing Sister Marie Regina, who ducked out of the way.

Sister Pauline's last day was the day she sat on her bed in the dormitory, playing her violin and refusing to go to chapel.

Then there was the postulant from Queens who saw an apparition in the garden. She was discovered there early in the morning, kneeling in front of the Sacred Heart statue. Jesus spoke to her, it was reported. Soon her parents were contacted and an ambulance dispatched her to St. Anne's Hospital. I learned this at night recreation from Jeanne, who never missed a detail of juicy gossip.

"Didn't you ever see her taking the apple cores out of the pit bowl and eating them?" she asked. "She thought she was St. Theresa."

"No," I said, "I never saw that." (At table I always had my eyes cast down, and anyway I was in a perpetual dreamlike state).

We had bath schedules—half an hour, twice a week. "When you wash don't look at your body or take pleasure in touching yourselves," Mother Consolata told us. We learned that a decade or so earlier, the sisters had been required to wear sateen coverings when they bathed so they would not be tempted to look at their bodies.

The half-hour bath time started when we went to the dormitory to change. We had to be bathed and dressed within that time frame. When I asked for shampoo, Mother said, "You don't need shampoo. Soap is plenty good enough."

The five-forty rising bell began our day. "Get up as if the bed were on fire," Mother told us.

There were prescribed silent prayers to say on rising. We dressed under our billowy granny gowns for modesty and kissed each part of the habit as we put it on. Twenty minutes to dress and make our beds before chapel.

Frequently I slept through the rising bell, and because in the dorm, our cubicles had curtains drawn, no one seemed to notice that I didn't get up. Whatever subconscious message my body was giving me went unheeded. When I awakened I scrambled to dress and went off to the chapel. As I passed Mother's seat, she gave me a look of censure. I felt so ashamed and I wondered if she believed I'd stayed deliberately to catch a few extra winks. I knew the scolding would come later as it always did when Mother corralled me after breakfast.

Most of my corrections were about my taking too long to do my function. I tried to do everything perfectly—scrubbing the bathtub, cleaning the toilet, dusting the mopboards. Sometimes I swept the floor twice to make sure that I hadn't left a particle of dust. "Sister, you take too much time doing your function. I don't understand. The other postulants finish much faster."

"Yes, Mother." (No excuses.)

Another time she told me that I must report to her when my function was finished. If our work was a prayer to offer to God, I ought to make it perfect, but how could I if I hadn't enough time?

Throughout my novitiate training I was often in tears, and I think I cried from nerves. Mother would say, "Stop that crying and be a woman."

Once when I had a migraine headache, I asked her for an aspirin. (We were not allowed to keep bottles of medicine and had to ask for what we needed.) She said, "Jesus Christ was crowned with thorns, and you want an aspirin!"

Yet, in spite of her somewhat austere manner, I respected her, admired her, and even loved her. One thing about Mother Consolata—she held herself to the same strict observance that she demanded from her novices.

I was drawn to the spiritual life, but sometimes I was overwhelmed by it all. A sudden notion to leave would come over me like a tidal wave. I felt so engulfed by the prospect of a life of continual self-abnegation that I thought of running away. I was drowning in a sea of blackness.

"Mother, I can't live this life," I said. "I want to leave now."

"Do you want to turn your back on God?" Her demeanor grew stern, almost hostile, and her words cut to the heart.

I felt like an ingrate…a traitor.

"No, Mother, I don't want to turn my back on God," I said.

"Then don't. This is a temptation, Sister. The harder it is, the more you have to offer."

She put her thumb on my forehead in a blessing. "I'll pray for you, Sister."

Novices and postulants were disappearing from our midst. One day they were there and the next day—gone, vanished. It was unsettling because the way we found out was by observing an empty chair in the refectory or noticing someone's vacant place in the chapel. In the silence I read anxiety and distress on the faces of other postulants. But we were not at liberty to discuss our feelings.

At instruction time Mother would make an announcement like: "Sister Violet left today. She didn't have a true vocation."

There would then be a collective sucking in of breath. Whenever anyone left, it filled me with profound sadness. Sister Violet gone! Not a chance to say good-bye, to wish her well. It was like a death in the family, the difference being that if a loved one dies in your family, you can talk about it and weep.

"Sisters, do not discuss this among yourselves. God has other plans for Violet. And don't try to get in contact with her. Put your trust in the Sacred Heart."

I could only mourn the loss of Sister Violet in my heart.

Sometimes I wished that I would be sent home like Violet or some of the others. "Maybe I don't have a true vocation," I told Mother one day, hoping she would agree with me.

"You have a very strong vocation, Sister. Pray for perseverance."

At such times I'd go to the chapel to pray. The chapel at St. Helena's was modern, with blonde wood benches and floor-to-ceiling windows that let in light. All was quiet except for the sound of candles flickering in votive glasses. Kneeling there in front of the tabernacle, gradually I'd feel a cloud lift and it seemed that I was surrounded by an aura. I believe I hypnotized myself into a state of euphoria, believing this was the life God wanted for me.

Every first Sunday of the month we had a day of recollection. It was like a retreat day—no talking at all, no recreation. The Blessed Sacrament was exposed on the altar in the gold monstrance. We took turns kneeling in the chapel for adoration, and all day there was a stream of sisters going in and out of the chapel. The purpose of this retreat was to give pause so that we could focus on our spiritual lives. Often some of the readings in the chapel spoke of death and dying. "What thoughts will come to you on your deathbed?" one passage asked. At eighteen, death seemed remote, and the images of the deathbed that were read out of those ancient tomes were frightening to me.

We retired earlier on those days, and sometimes in the

spring I'd hear birdsong outside my window and think how cheery those creatures sounded in contrast to how I was feeling in the midst of the gloom and doom.

I don't mean to give the impression that life in the novitiate was one of complete abnegation. There were times of levity as well. In good weather we took recreation out of doors, and once I remember finding an old rusted hand plow in the barn. I sat on it and when another novice grabbed hold of the handle to give me a ride, the plow fell apart. I fell on the ground amid howls of laughter from the others.

Mother reprimanded me for failing in the spirit of poverty—breaking community property and dismissing it so lightly. But that was one time I didn't feel guilty, and it was worth the scolding to have some fun.

One night, at instructions, Mother Consolata told us that a benefactor had donated several boxes of corsets that would be on display in the community room. There was tacit permission for us to take one for personal use. Corsets, I wondered. What would we want with them? The only time I'd seen a corset was when my grandmother asked me to assist her in pulling the pink strings of her corset around the bedpost to rein in her ample girth. Heavens! Even my mother didn't wear one.

Later in the community room, there was an atmosphere of Filene's Basement as a swarm of novices jostled and pushed to get at the bounty. I watched them open up the long white rectangular boxes and spill the sea of salmon—complete with strings and stays—onto the table.

Holding the garments up and measuring the lengths to their torsos, they appeared delighted with the prospect of girding themselves in this attire. After they'd laid claim to the garments, they folded them and tucked them back into the boxes that bore the trademark CAMP, before departing with their treasures. The novices would have to ask to keep the corsets, but because Mother had made them available, there was evidence of tacit permission.

Several days later Mother Consolata mentioned the merits of wearing a Camp corset. "It supports your back," she said, "when you're doing heavy lifting."

We'd been moving iron bed frames from the barn with Sister Therese Gertrude, who, despite her diminutive size, seemed to have the strength of an ox. I entertained the idea of wearing a corset, but by then, all had been taken.

When my mother came on the next visiting day, I asked if she would get me something. "I'd like you to get me a Camp corset," I said.

"What? Have you lost your mind? You're eighteen years old, and you're not going to corset yourself in whale bones!"

"Please, Mom," I begged. But my mother was adamant. "No corsets. I'll bring you a panty girdle the next time I come."

When I reflect on my state of mind at that time, I ask myself: Why did I want that nineteenth-century relic? Was it to identify with the novices, my role models? Or was it a metaphor for how I was girding myself for the religious life? I think a little of both.

We were being steeped in the Rule. We had to memorize the articles and recite them by heart—like catechism. A portion of the nightly instruction time was devoted to this exercise.

"When addressing one another, they will avoid the use of the *tutoyer,* unless, by the use of the *vouvoyer* they give offense to a sister who is a family member."

I am paraphrasing this article of the Constitutions. It's essentially correct as I remember it. For us American girls the rule was not relevant, since it referred to the French custom of using the familiar form of *you,* and the only English equivalent would be *thou,* which no one uses. Keeping in mind that the Congregation was founded in France in the 1800s, this rule was there to discourage familiarity among the sisters.

Another rule forbade *particular friendships.* These were characterized as exclusive friendships between two sisters. With the rule of silence, there was not much opportunity to forge friendships, but at recreation when sisters were laughing and talking, sometimes walking outside, it was inevitable that we would be drawn to some personalities. I was particularly fond of Sister Catherine Michael and

Sister Kathleen Joseph. Frequently I walked with them or sat next to them at recreation. Mother Consolata's eye was on us. "Sister," she said to me on more than one occasion, "I notice you sitting next to Sister Kathleen Joseph a lot. You need to mix in more."

What a travesty that there was an injunction against something so normal and natural as friendships. The vigilance about this, though I didn't realize it at the time, was to guard against suspected lesbian relationships.

"You've given your hearts to Christ," Mother Consolata said. "Don't take back any part of your gift." It was, she told us, one of the refinements of the vow of chastity that we were preparing to take. From my recollection many of us had a *connection* with one or more of the novices, but I took all the admonitions to heart. I tried not to think how much I loved Sister Catherine Michael or Sister Kathleen Joseph.

I was starving for reading, but we were not allowed any books other than *The Imitation of Christ* or *Lives of the Saints*. One day Mother Consolata's suitcase was in the hall and I knew that she was getting ready to depart for a weekend conference in South Bend. I seized my opportunity. I'd been longing to sit in that warm spot in the sunroom and take down one of the books from the shelves there. As soon as she left, I went straight to the sunroom and selected a poetry anthology that I opened to "The Lake Isle of Inisfree."

Yeats' lines spoke to me. I sat down on the wicker sofa in front of the picture window. The room was bathed in light and the sun's rays had already warmed the settee's cushions. I snuggled into them and read:

> And I shall have some peace there, for peace comes dropping slow
> Dropping from the veils of the morning to where the cricket sings
> There midnight's all a glimmer, and noon a purple glow,
> And evening's full of the linnet's wings.

> I will arise and go now, for always night and day
> I hear lake water lapping with low sounds by the shore
> While I stand on the roadway, or on the pavements grey
> I hear it in the deep heart's core.

In my "deep heart's core," I shall have peace there.

Brusquely the front door opened. In an instant Mother Consolata stood there.

"Sister, what are you doing here?"

She made the *tsk tsk* sound that was her customary way of chiding.

"Oh, I...I..."

"Go to the cellar, Sister, and offer yourself in the laundry. You know you're not supposed to be here."

Yes, my soul was longing for a little inspiration, but by choosing this meditation, outside the parameters, I had committed a transgression.

"Yes, Mother," I said. And I skulked away to the cellar like a beaten dog.

In the novitiate we learned that to deny ourselves little pleasures was one of the roads to sanctification. We could take our tea without sugar or eat more of a dish we didn't like. We could do a kind act for a disagreeable person. Anything that went against the grain was an opportunity to offer up.

My role model for this was Willy Doyle, Father William Doyle, SJ, an Irish chaplain in World War I. I found his autobiography in the book stacks at the Normal School while waiting to attend class. As I read about his life, I was completely captivated by his generosity of spirit and capacity for sacrifice. I found that his way was simple, based on small acts. Following his example, on certain days I'd eat bread without jam or butter, take less of some food I liked, eat more of the stringy beef that we got from government surplus. Once I swallowed whole bites of apple dumpling without chewing so as not to taste the syrupy cinnamon sauce that I liked.

I tried harder to be helpful to sisters I did not like. I kept a little notebook for this purpose and noted down my daily offerings.

After a while I looked for more ways to go against the grain. Willy Doyle's mantra was "Say *yes* to your *no* and *no* to your *yes*." There was an in-ground swill bucket in the yard at St. Helena's that had to be emptied at intervals. Under the hinged lid the sight of the maggot-covered garbage was disgusting. I volunteered to clean the bucket and, because it was so repulsive, I borrowed another idea from Father Doyle. I bound myself under pain of mortal sin to do it.

It is virtuous to do a disagreeable task that no one else wants to do or to help someone in need. But in this case I think I practiced self-deception, probably thinking myself holy because of my little heroic acts. And swallowing food without enjoying its taste is crazy. But that is how I was then.

I looked forward to the weekly interviews with Mother Consolata. I discussed my spiritual life and bared my soul to her. I read John of the Cross and Theresa of Avila. They were the saints who appealed to me because of their mysticism, and I wanted to emulate them so that I could have a more perfect union with Christ. I knew I could not compare myself to those saints, but reading about their struggles, the dark night of the soul, I felt I had found something in them that spoke to me.

When our founder, Jean-Baptiste Debrabant, wrote the Constitutions, he did not ordain the discipline (self-flagellation) prescribed by other religious orders. He believed that since teaching was the mission of the Congregation, the sisters should maintain their health in order to be more effective in their profession. Neither did we have the penance, common to some orders, of prostrating ourselves on the refectory floor and begging for food.

Mother Consolata allowed one penance. It was to kneel on the floor and extend our arms out in the form of a cross for about ten minutes. I did that frequently, kneeling beside my bed. I thought the more penance I did, the holier I would become.

Why did I feel this thirst for self-abnegation? I believe it was because I was young and impressionable, and I wanted to follow the example of our charismatic leader. It was probably the same dynamic that overtakes idealistic young people joining a cult.

Nevertheless, I had periodic doubts about my vocation. Each time I approached Mother Consolata, she would say, "This is a temptation. The devil does not want you to serve Our Lord. The stronger your vocation, the more the devil tries to tempt you to give up."

On each occasion such as this, overwhelmed by the rigidity of the life and the seeming relentlessness of it all, I was filled with desolation and despair. The prospect of spending a lifetime of denial seemed too impossible. Yet, whenever I told Mother Consolata that I wanted to leave, her counsel was for me to pray—to pray for a more generous spirit, to pray for the grace to serve Him who had called me.

"I will pray for you, too, Sister." And then she would trace the sign of the cross on my forehead.

The days of my postulancy passed like that, with my feeling alternately depressed and happy. Since it was not allowed to discuss these matters with any of the postulants and novices, the only ones I could unburden myself to were Mother Consolata, Reverend Mother Gabriel, and my confessor.

I told Father Sugrue in the confessional that I'd stopped believing in God.

"Here I am, Father. I'm a postulant, and I have doubts about the existence of God."

"Why, it's only natural, Sister," he said. "Here you're surrounded by so much religion. Be patient with yourself. This will pass."

"Maybe it will, Father, but I have doubts about my vocation, too. At times I just want to run out of here."

"Tell me, Sister, did you always like being around nuns?"

"Oh, yes, Father. Very much."

"Now you see, Sister, I think this is a sign that you belong here. I think you'd have a very hard time in the world. I'll pray for you, Sister. Now, for your penance say one *Our Father* and three *Hail Marys… Ego te absolvo…*"

Mother Gabriel Clare's office was at the top of the stairs at St. Helena's. She sat at a large oak rolltop desk, and most of the time her door was open. As provincial superior, Mother Gabriel Clare was in charge of maintaining the spiritual and temporal welfare of all the sisters in the province. Her responsibilities were diverse. When a sister died or another became ill, Mother Gabriel Clare would have to determine a solution for replacing them in the classroom. There were fiscal concerns, also. It took money to run the novitiate. We'd given in a minimal dowry sum when we entered, but that was not enough to pay for food, heat, and electricity. We postulants and novices did not earn money. The only revenue generated from the novitiate came from making unleavened hosts that were used for Mass. These would be sent out to various parishes for a fee.

Still, with all of her cares, Reverend Mother Gabriel always greeted me with a cheery smile. Many times when I happened to be at St Helena's, doing a function, I'd look in to see her there at that desk. "Excuse me, Reverend Mother," I'd say.

"Come in, Marion." She always dropped the *Sister,* calling me by my given name. "And how are you getting on, Marion?"

There was a presence about her that was calming, and though she was not physically attractive, I found that after being with her for a few minutes, she began to look beautiful. Instead of regarding her uneven features, I focused on her gaze. Her eyes, blue as cornflowers, met mine in a warm embrace.

I had many impromptu visits with her and I knew she liked me. When I talked with her, it was like visiting my grandmother.

On one occasion when I told her about doubting my vocation, I was so touched by her solicitude that I began to cry and could not stop myself. I think all the pent-up sorrow in me was released as if a valve had been loosened from deep inside. From her big pocket, under the habit, she produced a large white handkerchief and gave it to me. Then she took out a vial of tiny white pills, emptying the contents into the palm of her hand. "Take these, Marion," she said. "You know it all comes out of the ground."

I took the handkerchief and the pills. "Thank you, Reverend Mother," I said.

It was long after that visit that I learned the little white pills were phenobarbital.

As I said, we spent a great portion of the day engaged in manual work, and when we had finished our assigned housekeeping duties, or *functions,* we assisted in the cellar work in a variety of tasks that included washing clothes, hanging them on the line, and ironing.

The cellar was like a little factory with many different activities going on simultaneously. We entered from a door in the hallway and descended a flight of stairs.

There under two small windows was a double soapstone sink. Adjacent to the sink a rectangular wooden table, padded and covered with an old sheet, was for guimpe ironing. On the wall opposite the sink stood a cast-iron cook stove with an elbow-shaped metal vent. Near the stove, on the cement floor were several galvanized metal tubs—one containing the community black stockings, soaking in sudsy water. Another was filled with soiled handkerchiefs, waiting in bleach water to be boiled on top of the stove.

The cellar was a dim place with covered pipes overhead and sixty-watt bulbs hanging from the ceiling. On warm days we opened the bulkhead doors to let in more light. On the windowsills over the washtubs were gallon jugs containing water and scraps of leftover soap. The soap gradually dissolved into the slimy brown liquid that we used to wash the clothes in the old Maytag. Barrel-shaped and open, we could watch our underwear, handkerchiefs, sheets, pillowcases, and towels swirling around in a maelstrom. The Maytag made a whirring noise as its agitator swiveled back and forth, to and fro. We fed the finished wash, a few pieces at a time, through the machine's attached wringer, turning the crank to squeeze out the water.

We moved about silently, like a colony of ants, each of us engaged in some aspect of the cellar work. In this quiet atmosphere the only sounds came from the rhythmic sloshing of the washing machine, the gurgling of liquid from slop tubs emptying into the drain, the occasional thud of an iron pounding down hard on a guimpe.

Sometimes a novice would begin a litany: "Sacred Heart of Jesus…" Then a chorus of voices would respond, "…have mercy on us."

"Sacred Heart of Jesus…have mercy on us."

"Sacred Heart of Jesus…have mercy on us."

The endless repetition—just as in the cellar at the Prospect Street Convent.

I preferred silence to the rote prayers, so I didn't join in. But one day Yvette, who seemed to have converted from the cigarette-smoking, gum-chewing postulant into a sanctimonious zealot, looked at me and muttered, "Pagan."

I laughed. I thought it was very funny coming from her.

To say that the two most disagreeable tasks in the washing department were the stockings and handkerchiefs would be an understatement. Even after a good soaking in the tub, the bouquet of fifty or sixty sweaty stockings was enough to turn the stomach. The odor lingered even after the soak water had been dumped. But if the olfactory sensibilities were assaulted by the ripe stockings, nothing was as loathsome as the stink of the handkerchiefs. The fetid stench and disgusting sight of swirling mucous made me want to vomit. The handkerchiefs were stirred in their pot on top of the stove with a long, wooden stick as the water gradually heated up to the boiling point. Then the repulsive liquid was poured down the drain and the slimy handkerchiefs transferred to the Maytag.

Three or four novices stood at the padded table ironing the linen guimpes. That part of the habit consisted of a collar and bib and required heavy starching to maximize stiffness. The guimpes, like the bands, went through a two-stage starch ritual. First hot, then cold. The art of turning out a presentable guimpe resided in heating the iron to the right temperature. Too hot and it would scorch. Not hot enough—the guimpe would crumple. I thought it curious that the novices rubbed old beeswax candles on the irons to remove starch buildup on the irons. But it worked.

In the boiler room adjacent to the laundry, we made soap. A large galvanized tub was filled with fat, saved from the kitchen. A dose of lye was added and the mixture was stirred with a wooden paddle until it thickened like a pudding. After it solidified we cut it into soap bars that we used in the laundry.

Advent came—the penitential season observed in the Church for the four weeks preceding the anniversary of the birth of Christ. In the chapel all of the statues were draped with purple broadcloth. It was a rubric followed by Catholic places of worship all over the world—a reminder that, before the birth of the Savior, the world was in darkness.

In accordance with the season we were permitted no

letters from the outside. We were encouraged to redouble our efforts at mortification—taking less dessert, doing without sugar in our tea, and making other such small sacrifices.

During Advent, at Mass, the priest wore violet—with one exception. On the third Sunday of Advent—*Gaudete Sunday*— the purple robes were exchanged for rose-colored vestments signifying *joy*—a reminder that the penitential season of Advent was nearing the end—a kind of hiatus. On that day flowers could adorn the altar.

December twentieth, 1952, was my nineteenth birthday. It was a day without fanfare because, in the convent, name days—not birthdays—were the *cause celebre*. The only other person who knew it was my birthday that day was Mother Consolata. She knew it because, at about ten o'clock in the morning, the doorbell rang and a young man from Buffington's Florist arrived with a large white box under his arm.

The box, addressed to me and opened by Mother Consolata, was a present from my father. I remember the anguished look on Mother Consolata's face. She showed me the long-stem pink roses, still enveloped in their green floral tissue.

"Sister, you know it's still Advent and you're not supposed to get presents. I think we'll save these for the altar on Gaudete Sunday."

"Yes, Mother," I said.

I was happy that my flowers would decorate the altar on Sunday, but it was my birthday that day. As Mother Consolata took the flower box away, I thought of my father and how he would be anticipating my surprise. It made me sad—more for him than for me.

A few days before Christmas, Mother Consolata called me out of the cellar. I followed her into the classroom, wondering why I'd been summoned. What had I done or not done?

She turned to me. "Sister," she said, "you know you're not allowed to have visitors during Advent!"

I was listening to her, but I was puzzled because I already knew that we couldn't have visitors.

"Your mother is in the parlor, Sister. She asked to see you because your father is in the hospital."

"My father…in the hospital?"

"Yes, I've made an exception, Sister. But don't stay too long."

My mother was weeping when I went into the parlor. "Your father has pneumonia," she said. "I'm so worried about him."

I tried to console my mother and to mask my sadness at hearing that my father was sick. "How serious is it?"

"I don't know yet. I'll see the doctor this afternoon."

I stayed with my mother as long as I dared, and then escorted her to her car. I hated to see her go like that, and it took a piece out of my heart to know that my father was sick in the hospital.

When I went back in, I reported the news about my father.

"I'll pray for him, Sister."

"Thank you, Mother," I said.

It occurred to me that a little human kindness might have consoled my mother and me more than a promised prayer.

On Christmas Eve we postulants were sent to bed early—about seven o'clock. We knew that the novices were preparing something special for us. When I got to my cubicle in the dorm, I found that the pillow on my bed had been decorated with sprigs of spruce and cut-out angels salvaged from old Christmas cards. Such a simple thing, but it seemed a nice gesture on the part of the novices and it made me feel happy. I was also looking forward to the Midnight Mass, for which we'd rehearsed *Hodie Christus Natus Est—Today Christ Is Born.*

After I'd washed and gotten into bed, one of the novices appeared with a mug of hot mulled wine—the first wine I'd had since entering. I took the cup from her and tasted the beverage. It was sweet like honey and I drank it down in sips. I must have gone to sleep right after that, and I was awakened some time later by the sound of Christmas carols (from records) and a concert of bells. It all seemed so magical.

Our parents were not permitted to visit with us on

Christmas Day—so that we could spend time with the religious community—but we were allowed to talk all day. I know it was disappointing for my parents not to see me at Christmas. Phone calls were allowed, and I was glad to know that my father was out of the hospital. I remember saying, "Dad, Christmas in the convent is even more special than it would be outside."

"Just remember you wouldn't be there if it weren't for us," my father said. He sounded vexed, but I realized he was feeling hurt and sad.

I wished I could have retracted my insensitive remark.

As postulants we were in the probationary stage, preparing to take the next step in our religious formation. The Mother General and her councilors in Rome would vote to admit or reject us based on the reports sent by our novice mistress.

If admitted, we would be clothed in the novice habit on the feast of the immaculate heart of Mary, the twenty-second day of August.

Each of us was required to write a letter to Reverend Mother Marie Therese, the general superior, expressing our sincere desire to serve God in this holy state. Handwriting had to be practiced until it approached perfection in Mother Consolata's eyes. There was a form to follow, and we wrote the letters on stationery that had the embossed hearts of Jesus and Mary.

On taking the habit, we would no longer be called by our secular names, but by saints' names. We were asked to list three religious names in order of priority in case our first choice was already taken. Mother Consolata told us not to reveal our choices.

The idea of dressing in the habit and being called Sister *Something* was quite appealing to all of us, it seemed. The fact that our admission was not a given, that we had to be deemed worthy of it, I think, added weight to our own decision making.

In the meantime we sewed the habits that we would wear on Clothing Day. In the scripture Jesus said it was easier for a camel to pass through the eye of a needle than for a rich man to enter the Kingdom of Heaven. Well, aside from riches, I think it would have been easier for some of us postulants to scrub and wax ten floors than to master the art of sewing the parts of the habit.

It took twenty/twenty vision to poke cotton thread through the eye of the skinny number ten needle, and nimble fingers to push the needle in and out of the material. Tiny stitches were called for, especially on the bands.

"Rip it out," said Sister Therese Gertrude.

What a lot of stitching! Narrow strips of thin batiste had to be gathered and sewn to a tape. The raw edge was turned in 1/16 of an inch, then rolled over and creased alongside the edge of a table. That done, we would thread our needles and begin hemming.

"Pass da needle true in a slant," said Sister Therese Gertrude.

She was born in America, but never lost her French-Canadian accent.

The instruction theme was different every night. Sometimes it was on obedience, other times on poverty or other points of the Holy Rule. The vow of chastity was treated as the renouncing of matrimony in lieu of becoming the bride of Christ. Each of us was called by God, and a vocation was nothing to be trifled with.

"Don't look back at the fleshpots of Egypt" was one of Mother Consolata's favorite sayings. Whenever I thought I'd made a mistake in choosing this life, I'd recall those words, taken from the Old Testament. I felt ashamed for calling my vocation into question.

We had few lectures on the vow of chastity. What Mother Consolata told us was that the vow of chastity would get easier as we got older. "You've given your lives to God. Don't take back your gift by forming attachments to other persons or objects."

Marriage was elevated to the status of a sacrament for the procreation and raising of children. The concept of two loving people giving themselves to each other and enjoying sex was not even mentioned because, according to the Church's teaching, *sex merely for the pleasure* was sinful.

Masturbation was a mortal sin, although Mother

Consolata never used that word—I think the closest she came was "Don't take pleasure in your own body." Lesbianism was never mentioned—as if saying that word out loud was redolent with shame.

There was only the admonition against "particular friendships." Mother Consolata watched us like a hawk to track how often we sat next to the same sister at recreation. Well, it was the only legitimate time to talk, and naturally, we liked to sit with those who attracted us by personality or ideas.

The novitiate was the training ground where the novice mistress tested our mettle. I remember that she told us, once, the advice given to her by a priest of the Redemptorist Order: "Bounce them hard, Mother," he'd told her.

And so she did.

Our lives as postulants continued in our daily observance of the Rule, the prayers, chanting the Office, and fulfilling our domestic chores. Usually at noon recreation we walked up and down in the tennis court on the premises. During evening recreation we took our workbaskets to the community room, where, during that hour, we sewed as we talked. We darned stockings and patched underwear. We sewed the merino dresses and serge shawls that we would wear as novices.

The months passed. On August thirteenth we went on the retreat that would culminate on the twenty-second day, the feast of the Immaculate Heart of Mary, our Clothing

Day. Although we'd been accustomed to keeping silence daily, we had not experienced the silence of the retreat. During those ten days there was no recreation. In addition to all of the daily prayer rubrics, we were required to attend several sessions a day in the chapel, listening to the homilies of the retreat priest. The purpose of the talks was to motivate us to imitate the life of Christ, but also to obey the Holy Rule of our Congregation. The retreat priest reminded us of our temporal lives and said that no matter how great our sufferings in this life, we would be rewarded in the next. "Imagine your deathbed," he said, "and ask yourself if you will be ready to meet your heavenly Bridegroom." We were encouraged to make a general confession of our sins—that meant re-confessing any sins of the past.

Finally August twenty-second arrived. On this day we would become novices and take the habit of the Congregation. Prior to the retreat we had rehearsed the ceremony in the chapel, processing up the aisle, sometimes accompanied by organ music, carrying pretend candles in our hands. We had practiced reciting the formula that we would say before the bishop. I remembered the words from the ceremony day when I entered. We practiced it all, including kneeling on the steps of the sanctuary. As we knelt there, our group of nine postulants would listen to the bishop.

"My daughters, what do you ask?"

"Your Excellency, we ask to be admitted to the Congregation of the Holy Union of the Sacred Hearts."

"And is it of your own free will that you ask this?"

"It is our desire, Your Excellency, and may God perfect it in His mercy."

More formulaic prayers followed. We renounced Satan and renewed our Baptismal vows. I suppose the bishop then said something like, "Go in peace, my daughters."

We stepped down and crossed to the right-hand side of the sanctuary, where Sister Therese Gertrude stood beside the wicker basket of newly blessed habits. She handed each of us a folded ensemble—the clothes we would put on and wear as newly minted novices. The organ music recommenced and we stepped down from the altar steps, proceeding up the aisle. We supported our black bundles, as I recall, on our arms, and I do not remember what became of the lighted candles. But now our noviceship was beginning. In the community room across from the chapel, Sister Rosalie was waiting.

Again (it had been a year since she'd dressed me in the postulant veil) I felt Sister Rosalie's touch as she placed the guimpe around my neck and fastened it with a collar button. It felt like a plate of armor.

The crinkly band encircling my face cut off my vision like a horse blinder. I wondered what I looked like, but there were no mirrors. Meanwhile, the other postulants were being dressed—some by a favorite nun who had sponsored them, as in my case.

There were only whispered utterances: "Turn… Hold still… Let me see… Hmm." We were still on retreat. Sister Rosalie and I communicated with our eyes. She seemed pleased to see me in the habit. Everyone looked…like *nuns*!

We lined up to go back into the chapel. Bearing the weight of the heavy serge shawl on my back, and unable to move my neck in the stiff collar, I felt as if I'd been poured into a straitjacket. A lighted candle with its cardboard bobeche was placed in my hand, and I held it almost unconsciously. We moved out of the clothing room and into the nave of the chapel. Up, up the aisle, processing slowly to the rhythm of the organ chords, we reached the altar gate and ascended the steps to the sanctuary.

The bishop rose from his chair, ready to confer our names. The organ music ceased, and I could sense that the reverential silence was ratcheted up even more.

Norajean knelt on the sanctuary step as the bishop stood before her, reading her new name from a card. "Receive, Sister, your name in religion: Sister Magdalena Maria."

I was next. "Receive…Sister Marion Joseph…"

The name had been my first choice. *Joseph* was for my father, his confirmation name. "Please don't take *Leo*," he'd said.

Now the organ intoned the first notes of the Gregorian hymn, *Veni, Creator Spiritus* (Come, Holy Spirit), and the entire congregation took up the chant. It was my favorite Gregorian chant. After we'd received our names, we stepped down from the sanctuary and approached Reverend Mother Gabriel Clare, who stood in front of Blessed Mother's statue. There each of us, in turn, made a profound bow to Reverend Mother, signifying our obedience to the Rule. I remember Mother Gabriel Clare embracing me and smiling as if to say, "You made it." Then she handed me my own copy of the Holy Rule. It was the first time I'd had the thin black book in my hands.

After Bridey, newly named Sister Bridgetta Marie, took her place in the pews, the congregation broke into the *Te Deum* (Praise God). Then there followed the Congregation's hymn to commemorate the spirit of the Order.

The rule of silence was suspended for the day, and all was jubilation in the corridors as we neophyte novices exited the chapel. The professed sisters wanted to get a look at us and ask again about our names. This was one day when we were free to mingle with the nuns. Sister Rosalie hugged me and straightened my band.

I was in such a euphoric state that I cannot remember what we said to each other. All I know is that I felt a step closer to becoming a real Sister like her.

The noon bell rang and all talking ceased. We stood still, reciting the Angelus prayers—*The angel of the lord*

*declared unto Mary and she conceived of the Holy Ghost.
Hail Mary, full of grace, the Lord is with thee…*

How we must all have believed that *taking the habit*
would confer on us a new identity. Our Congregation did
not have the custom of veiling its novices in white. On
Clothing Day, in our black veils, we were indistinguishable
from the professed. We wore the silver cross, engraved
with the emblems of our Congregation and the name:
Holy Union of the Sacred Hearts.

What a thrill it was to hear the novice mistress ask,
"Where is Sister Magdalena Maria? Sister Bridgetta Marie?
Sister Marion Joseph?" We rushed to inspect the func-
tion and bath lists so we could see our names in print.
Putting off the old man and putting on the new—Saint
Paul to the Ephesians. Often we'd read this quote in the
New Testament, and we'd heard it from the lips of Mother
Consolata until it was ingrained in us. Yes, we'd left our old
selves behind. Enveloped in this black nineteenth-century
dress, our identities were concealed, submerged, annihi-
lated. Death to worldliness. Brides of Christ.

I had entered what was called my canonical year.
Secular studies were suspended, and emphasis was on
spiritual formation. We spent our days, much as before,
doing manual work and reading books on the spiritual life.
We memorized the articles of the Holy Rule and continued to recite them at nightly instruction.

The Bride of Christ now, I desired to attain communion with my Beloved. I savored the quiet time for contemplation, although at times, I'd be suddenly seized with the desire to escape the regimentation. Once again, on these occasions when the prospect of a whole lifetime of sacrifice seemed unbearable, I'd confide my thoughts to Mother Consolata.

"It's a temptation, Sister."

Yes, always it was a temptation and always, the same advice: "Go and pray, Sister."

I prayed. I read the Canticle of Canticles:

"Show me, O Thou whom my soul loveth, where Thou feedest, where Thou liest in the midday… Thy cheeks are beautiful as the turtledoves…a cluster of cypress is my love to me… Behold Thou art fair my love, Thine eyes are those of doves…"

Mother Consolata had given all of us a small print, an artist's rendition of Christ, the man. The face of Jesus was very handsome, but very effeminate, with long hair parted in the middle cascading over a white tunic. The expression of the face was gentle and the eyes, soft brown, reflected light.

The picture was also an optical illusion because if you stared long enough at the forehead, you would see a chalice with a host suspended above it. Mother Consolata, herself, was very fond of looking at the print and watching to see the chalice appear.

I kept this picture in my prayer book and looked longingly at the image of Jesus. I was the Bride of Christ.

I was naïve and romantic, a perfect candidate for manipulation. As teenagers we were vulnerable, and more so because of the enclosed environment and the daily exhortations from our novice mistress.

Sublimation was the word! Mother Consolata told us, without even mentioning *sexual desire,* that through the vow of chastity, we would sublimate our need for human attachments.

I am not saying that there was any malevolence on the part of our novice mistress. I believe she was so indoctrinated from her own training that she believed everything she taught us, however unenlightened it was.

In love with an illusion, I spent the next two years in the novitiate, alternately devoting myself to the life and questioning my vocation. At the end of the canonical year, Mother Consolata told me that she and Reverend Mother, after serious consideration, were sending me to teach part time in the little academy.

I was thrilled at the prospect of teaching in the same school that I'd attended as a boarder. I took charge of the class after morning recess until midday, teaching spelling and geography to a fourth-grade class of about twenty girls. The teaching seemed to be natural for me, and the little girls were sweet. I taught there for two months until the regular fourth-grade teacher returned in December.

In February Mother Consolata told me I was being assigned to teach third grade at the academy until the end of the school year. A sister had died and I was to replace her until the end of the year. My joy at being chosen was overshadowed by Mother's remark:

"If you flop on the job, we can get someone else."

I taught full time, and managed to correct papers and prepare lessons while still following the prayer schedule of the novitiate and attending the nightly instruction.

When school ended in June, I was only two months away from taking my first vows. The summer passed, and on August thirteenth we went on retreat in preparation for our profession. I listened to the homilies of the retreat priest. I knew it was a serious step to pledge myself to the three vows. Though, according to the rubrics of Canon Law, I would be bound by these vows for only one year, Mother Consolata told us not to think of it that way.

"When you take your vows," she said, "you are taking them for your whole life without reservation. Do you want to take back what you've offered?"

We practiced walking in procession for the ceremony, giving the responses to the bishop and kneeling on the altar steps, where we would say, *I, Sister ---, take for one year the vows of poverty, chastity, and obedience...*

On the night before profession I was seized, once again, with doubt about the awesome decision of committing my whole life to the convent. I went to Mother Consolata's room and knocked on the door. It was the time of the Grand Silence. The door opened, and I saw that Mother was already in her kimono and nightcap. She seemed surprised to see me there in the doorway.

I said, "Mother, I can't go through with this. I can't take vows tomorrow."

"Nonsense, Sister. This is the last temptation from the devil."

She blessed me, making the sign of the cross on my forehead with her thumb.

"Go now, and I'll pray for you."

The door closed and I was standing in the darkened hallway. I turned and went back to my dormitory, alone with my thoughts. Maybe it was normal to have doubts, I reflected, before making such a commitment. I recalled how my cousin Peggy, the night before her wedding, said to me, "I don't think I want to do this."

I knew that Peggy was deeply in love with Don, and I put her remark down to the wedding jitters. Maybe it was like that for me.

In the morning the rising bell woke me. My first thought was that this was the day. I dressed and went outside to the lineup. Dawn was breaking, and, in a similar way, I felt a new dawn breaking inside myself. Today I would be wed to my heavenly Bridegroom.

Black Horse Pike

Nine o'clock in the morning, and already I could tell it was going to be one of those dog days that hit around the middle of August. I stood alone outside the novitiate, waiting for the ride that would take me to my first mission. All nine of us had been assigned to different parish schools up and down the eastern seaboard. I was going to Mount Ephraim, New Jersey.

I paced the walkway in front of the turn-of-the century building that had been the home of a prominent family of florists before the Congregation purchased the estate. I had just completed three years of rigorous training under the aegis of my novice mistress, Mother Consolata, and I had pledged my vows. Now I was going to join the ranks of the other professed nuns. Full of religious fervor, I antici-pated the challenge of living up to the ideals that Mother Consolata had inspired in me. At the same time I was feel-ing the impending loss of my peers—the sisters in my set (in nun-parlance sets were groups that had entered on the same day). We'd transitioned together from giggly postulants to serious novices, and now—to neophyte nuns with vows. We were about to be dispersed to different convents and not see each other until summer, when we would convene for classes at our own college. The sweet part was that we had graduated and we were poised to begin our active teaching apostolate.

I glanced up at the front door as the sun played on its frosted glass window. I thought of how each morning we'd passed through this portal and lined up by seniority on the gravel path. In the blackness of pre-dawn winter days, we'd shivered in the cold, wrapping ourselves in our knitted shawls as we waited for the last ones to assemble. Two sharp clacks from Mother's hinged wooden clapper penetrated the silence and signaled us to move across the yard to St. Helena's Hall. Without hesitation the phalanx marched forward like a monolithic machine.

This is good-bye, I thought. *Tomorrow I won't be in the lineup with the novices.*

At the far end of the circular drive, my eyes took in the image of the old copper beech tree whose leaves reddened all summer long into a dark coppery tone by autumn. Next to the beech stood a gingko that dropped its fan-shaped leaves, like tiny presents, on the lawn. Good-bye to those friends, too.

The door opened and Mother Consolata came outside

just as a shiny white sedan pulled up to the entrance. The driver was a young woman with blond hair, a Mrs. Rafferty—as I would learn from the introduction—a volunteer-parishioner who'd come to chauffeur me to the New Jersey convent.

A skinny nun bounced out of the passenger side of the car and greeted Mother Consolata and me. She was Sister Olive Marie, named appropriately, I thought—for her wiry appearance put me in mind of Popeye's girlfriend, Olive Oyl. She had small brown eyes that darted everywhere, and her hands and feet moved in a kinetic dance.

"Well, good morning, Mother," she said, in what sounded to me like a Midwestern accent. "This the new sister?" she asked, half talking to herself.

Mother Consolata touched my forehead, etching the sign of the cross on my brow with her fingers. "Keep the Rule and it will keep you. God bless you, Sister."

I opened the rear door of the vehicle and slid onto the upholstered seat next to the window. As the motor started and the car began to pick up speed, we rolled across the gravel driveway, crunching the stones underneath. I cast a backward glance at the novitiate building. Mother Consolata had already gone inside, and I turned away. Sister Olive Marie craned her neck around from the front passenger side.

"Hey, kid, we're ridin' in a CHE VRO LAY! Whadya think?" She extended a pack of Wrigley's spearmint. "Want some gum?"

"No thanks, Sister," I said.

She turned to Mrs. Rafferty. "Okay. Might as well get going to that chicken farm in New Jersey."

"Chicken farm?" I said.

"Yeah, I got my billet-doux. Teaching seventh grade in the boonies. Ever hear of Swedesboro?"

"Hm," I said.

We'd been trained in the novitiate to accept everything as God's will. A change of teaching assignment, a move to a different convent—a good sister didn't complain.

Sister Olive Marie squirmed in her seat, twisting around to me to emphasize whatever she was saying. She was a verbal machine gun, and her steady stream of chatter was only punctuated by the masticating sounds of gum snapping and cracking.

I wondered what my novice mistress would have said about Sister Olive's demeanor, her liberal use of slang— so out of sync with the "religious decorum" of the novitiate. In my head I could hear Mother Consolata's lecture about worldly religious— nuns who slipped into secular ways and imitated people on the outside. "We have left the world behind," she would say, "and we are not of this world."

We stopped midway on our trip at a secluded tree-lined grove to eat our brown bag lunches. After we brushed away some debris from a picnic table, we sat down on the benches and opened up the lunch that our cook had prepared: tomato sandwiches, cheese and apples, and coffee in a thermos. The Rule proscribed the sisters from eating in the company of seculars. But, although I'd just emerged from the hothouse of spiritual training, I was not surprised that we made an exception for Mrs. Rafferty. After all, I thought, Mrs. Rafferty was giving up her time to drive us to New Jersey.

Sister Olive Marie acted like someone who'd suddenly been cured of lockjaw and needed to spew out a year's worth of talk. And though I was mindful of keeping the rule of silence, myself, it seemed common sense to suspend the rule for the sake of Mrs. Rafferty. After our small repast we resumed our trip through the long corridor of Connecticut, passing the outskirts of New York and making our way to the New Jersey Turnpike.

At about three o'clock in the afternoon, we turned onto a two-lane highway that I would come to know later as Black Horse Pike. Farther down on this same road, we approached a modest neighborhood of post-war houses, and Mrs. Rafferty maneuvered her Chevy into the narrow driveway of one of the nondescript dwellings. "Well, here we are," she said, cutting off the motor and pulling up the brake.

From my seat in the back of the vehicle, I stared through the open window at an undistinguished white-frame house set back on a sloping patch of parched grass. The convent? I mused.

It wasn't what I expected for a convent, but before I

had time to reflect, Sister Olive Marie leaped out of the car. "This is it, kid. C'mon, don't be a poke."

Mrs. Rafferty removed the ignition keys and picked up her purse. Both of us got out of the car, and together we walked up the driveway to the side of the house. Heat rose from the blacktop like a blast from the netherworld. My starched collar had already melted around the edges, and I was drenched in sweat.

As we approached the back stoop, Sister Olive Marie reached out to embrace another nun. The fluted white bands of their headdresses collided as the two inclined their heads, and you could hear the friction of starched linen. No kissing on the mouth. That was the way we sisters greeted each other after a journey. Sister Olive Marie looked up and gestured to the other nun. "Hey, Cousin, here's your youngster," she said, introducing me to my new superior. "Mother Inez Pauline…Sister Marion Joseph."

I wasn't sure if Sister Olive and Mother were blood relatives or if "cousin" was just another one of Sister Olive Marie's colloquialisms. I said, "Good to meet you, Mother."

Mother Inez Pauline gave me a steely look and turned to face Sister Olive Marie. They both laughed. No doubt, three years of formation had made their mark on me, and I probably appeared stiff and formal, but I felt hurt by Mother's cold reception. Mother Consolata wouldn't have treated anyone like that, I told myself.

Mother opened the screen door and we stepped inside

the green kitchen. A chrome and Formica-topped table with four matching chairs stood against the wainscoted wall. Cream-colored countertops matched the plastic surface of the table. Everything was immaculate, but I found it strange that there was not a crucifix or any other religious symbols that might have suggested a convent.

Immersed in my thoughts I revisited the novitiate kitchen, where I'd taken my turn washing up what we called the beat-ons (pots and pans) at the soapstone sink. A square oak table stood in the center of the room there, and the coal-black stove took up most of the space against the wall. A large crucifix hung in the space between the two windows that faced the veranda. I pictured the high ceilings of St. Helena's, the white walls, the corridors darkened by walnut paneling. Though in its heyday the house had belonged to a wealthy industrialist, and some of the vestiges from that era remained, we, nevertheless, lived very simply without superfluities. And I missed the Spartan comfort of that house on Rock Street.

But I scolded myself for this reverie. I walked on. The doorway from the kitchen led to the dining room, its space entirely given to a long, lace-covered table and mahogany chairs. A set of green Melmac dishes was set for twelve. Dinner plates, cereal bowls, and cups and saucers made out of indestructible post-war plastic—a contrast, I reflected, to the oilcloth-covered refectory tables laden with earthenware dishes at St. Helena's.

French doors separated the dining area from a room with a gold brocaded sofa and chintz-covered chairs. To the right of the dining room, a staircase led to the second story, and divided the house into two sections. To get to the other side, you had to step up onto a landing and then descend two steps to a room that ran the length of the house. The room had been subdivided into a community room and a chapel.

The community room was furnished with a long conference table and chairs, and in another space there were individual workstations for the sisters to prepare classes. Floral-patterned draperies had been drawn back on traverse rods, and Venetian blinds let in light through the wall of windows. The workstations were hinge-topped student desks.

Just past the desks a door led into the tiny chapel. I took holy water from the wall font and made the sign of the cross. Inside I genuflected and knelt at one of the prie-dieux. The familiar flicker of the wax candle burning inside the red sanctuary lamp comforted me. *Dear Lord,* I prayed, *if it is your will for me to be here, please give me the grace and the strength I need to persevere.*

I must have stayed there for several minutes. I was unsure of myself and I missed the familiar structure of the novitiate, the monastic simplicity and quietude of the place. I was homesick.

Sister Francine Therese, the sub-superior, escorted me to my sleeping quarters in the annex adjacent to the main house—a brown bungalow laid out like a railroad flat. We stepped up onto the little porch, and Sister turned the key in the lock that opened the door onto a room with white-painted walls and a floor covering of green linoleum. The room was furnished with a bed, a chest of drawers, and a nightstand. "This is your room," Sister Francine Therese said, "and this is the only entrance we use. The other sisters will pass through here at night and in the morning. Since you're the youngest…the rooms go by seniority."

She seemed to be apologizing for the inconvenience, but I was prepared for anything. Not so bad, I thought, compared to the novitiate dormitory where five of us had shared curtained cubicles.

The room faced north, and a window beside the bed let in dim afternoon light, but the space was small and had a low ceiling. I was glad that I would not be spending time here except to sleep. I unpacked my suitcase and put my clothes in the dresser.

In the days that followed, it was a relief to work in my classroom, preparing lessons for my fourth-grade students. Mother Inez Pauline did not seem to like me very much, and so I avoided her as much as possible. Whenever our paths crossed she found something to criticize.

She assigned me to the laundry. I was to wash the community clothes each day and hang them outside to dry.

Eager to carry out my function and be of service, I established a routine. Every morning, after I dressed, I went to the cellar and loaded the soiled garments into the automatic washer so they'd be ready to hang after breakfast. I felt that things were going well until one morning when Mother approached me before class. "Sister, from now on I want you to wait until Mass is finished to do the washing. The noise from the machine is distracting when we're in the chapel."

"Yes, Mother," I said.

The new regulation made it difficult to get the wash out before school began, but I hustled to the cellar right after breakfast. Sometimes when the priest was late arriving for Mass, I just about made the deadline. Sister Eileen offered to help me, but Mother told her that the laundry was my sole responsibility. About two weeks went by before there was an additional mandate. Mother called me aside one morning. "I want you to take the clothesline in from the yard every afternoon. People walking past... it...it doesn't look nice."

My immediate reaction to this requirement was that it made no sense. I couldn't imagine any passerby saying, "Oh, look, there's a clothesline in the nuns' backyard!" And I knew the extra time it would take me in the morning to string up the line would probably mean that I wouldn't finish hanging the clothes in time for class. But I was also mindful that, in the true spirit of obedience, I needed to submit my will.

"Yes, Mother," I said.

Of course it became a toss-up as to whether I should get the clothes on the line or get to school on time. I arrived late to school most of the time.

"You've failed in obedience again."

"Yes, Mother."

I compared Mother Inez Pauline to Mother Consolata—perfect antipodes. Mother Consolata was nearly six feet tall and as thin as Gandhi. She had an elongated face and high cheekbones. Her back was as straight as an iron rod, and she moved with the grace of a phantom. Although she was strict, she had a sense of humor and she was kind.

Mother Inez Pauline was short and rather round. Hooded lids over dark brown eyes gave her an exotic look, except when she distorted her lips and made a smarting sound with her tongue. Sensuality seeped through the layers of serge. I watched her undulating movements as she swished her hips side to side—her worldly walk so unlike Mother Consolata's stately stride. What were her secrets? She was a puzzle to me. I wondered if she really believed in the religious life.

Mother Inez Pauline seemed disingenuous. She appeared to observe the rubrics, but I sensed in her an air of falsity. I recalled an Emerson quotation, "What you are thunders so loud that I cannot hear what you say."

One morning, in the pre-dawn silence of the chapel—the only light coming from the sanctuary lamp on the altar,

I was absorbed in meditation. Suddenly, agh! Pain in my shoulder! I looked up, startled to see the black form of my superior hovering over me like a specter. Why did she punch me? She was grabbing onto me and pulling me out of my seat. We were tethered as she pushed me out of the chapel, through the community room, up over the landing. We were going fast through the refectory into the kitchen. Still holding on to me, she paused to open the cellar door and switch on the light.

As she thrust me forward, I was propelled downward at such speed I did not feel my shoes touching the steps. At once in the cellar she began shrieking like a banshee and shoving me toward the washing machine like an insane person. She opened the lid and grabbed the soiled clothes, flinging the pieces in rapid-fire—bloomers, bras, facecloths, and towels—all hurtling through the air like projectiles. The cellar was littered with balled-up pieces of underwear covered in detergent dust.

"Why do you wash all this (sic) clothes together? The… the…bras…the…the…towels! Don't you know how to do anything?"

Too shocked to react, I did not speak. I looked at her in supplication. When the outburst was over she turned away, and gathering the folds of her habit, she slowly ascended the stairs. I surveyed the mess around me, and in the act of picking up the scattered pieces of laundry, I regained my composure.

I suppose I must have returned to the chapel, and I can picture myself walking up to the front, genuflecting, and kneeling in place. I wonder how I was able to pray after that. But prayer was my refuge, and up until then I had felt quite safe in the chapel. Now even my private communion with God had been invaded. I tried to see God in my superior, but I wrestled with the temptation to see Mother Inez Pauline not as God's representative, but as my oppressor.

To Mother Inez Pauline my demeanor must have seemed strange. I suppose I appeared to her like a kind of zombie whenever she reprimanded me. I simply said, "Yes, Mother." I had been trained not to offer any explanation for my failings. "A good religious does not excuse herself." Often she mocked me in front of the other sisters. In a tone an octave above her normal speaking voice, she mimicked me. "Yes, Mother," she would say to anyone within earshot. Then, referring to me in the third person, she would add, "She's unconscious."

Tears welled up whenever she humiliated me, but I fought them back, not wanting to appear weak in front of her. I did my crying at night.

I had no allies in the community. It appeared that all of the sisters acted in ways to please Mother. I think everyone was afraid of her temper. There was no one I could trust and no one to give me counsel.

Mother Inez Pauline had a liaison with Jean Albarelli, a

high school girl who lived in the parish. Jean came to visit Mother every Saturday morning while the other sisters attended classes at Villanova. They'd sit at the kitchen table and Mother would call down to me in the cellar. "Sister, make Jean some coffee." Neither of them acknowledged my presence as I poured coffee into Jean's cup. They spoke to each other, ignoring me as if I were a servant. I thought it bizarre playing waitress to Mother's girlfriend.

Often Mother was absent from night prayers. At the conclusion of that exercise in the chapel, we observed the Grand Silence and went to our rooms. It was the time of strictest silence when we shut out all distraction and prepared for the next day's meditation. Speaking to anyone at that time was a grave infraction of the rule. Yet, on leaving the chapel, sometimes, I'd see a light on in the parlor behind the closed door. As I left the chapel to go to my room, I never knew who was in the parlor, but I suspected it was probably Jean.

The most physically beautiful nun was Sister Maureen Therese, the kindest in the community. She seemed to do everything perfectly in a quiet way, and her spare moments were spent in prayer. On more than one occasion, I caught Mother looking admiringly at Sister Maureen Therese.

One morning in mid-October, Sister Maureen's chair in the refectory was vacant. She was gone and everyone was stunned. No one talked about it in the open, but a kind of sub-current ran through the community. Sister Maureen

Therese, we learned, had been transferred to New York. Why now, after the school year had begun? I wondered. Transfers were generally made in August before the start of the school year. Mother seemed more moody than usual.

I intuited some connection between Mother Inez Pauline and Sister Maureen Therese. Why had Sister Maureen's room been in the main house near Mother Inez Pauline when she had less seniority than some of the others? I asked myself if Sister Maureen had requested the transfer. Not wanting to judge I dismissed these thoughts.

I often wondered about Mother Inez Pauline's background and what had motivated her to enter religion. She did not appear to be happy, and there seemed to be something artificial about her observance of religious rubrics. I wondered if she did not want to be in the convent, but felt herself trapped.

The more sarcastic my superior was with me, the more I retreated into myself. Her continual reminders of my failings robbed my confidence. When she came near me, I cringed, anticipating what cruel things she might say.

At table my body tensed. I trembled. I could not raise my coffee cup to my mouth unless I steadied it with two hands. I could hardly control my shaking, and I began to dread going to the refectory. As soon as I sat down at the table, the fear of being observed with evidence of shattered nerves took hold of me, and I shook even more.

We were obliged by the Rule to follow the same prayer

horarium as in the novitiate. We sang, in Latin, the psalms of the Little Office of the Blessed Virgin, part of the official prayer of the Church. We chanted *Prime, Terce, Sext* and *None,* the Canonical Hours that contemplative orders of nuns sing in the night. But because we were a teaching order and did not rise in the night to pray, we sang those hours in the morning.

From the first time, as a postulant, that I'd held the Office book in my hands, I'd loved singing the psalms. The Latin words seemed to meld together as our young voices soared upward and fell to a whisper at the end of each invocation. The undulating waves of sound that rose and fell from alternate sides of the chapel created a rhythm that was almost hypnotic.

In Mt. Ephraim we carried out the same rubric, chanting, rising for the antiphons, and bowing at the Gloria Patris. Sometimes while chanting I would scan the page for the English translation and find solace in the words of the poet.

> *God is our refuge and strength: our helper*
> *In troubles which have fallen on us heavily*
> *Therefore we shall not fear when the earth*
> *shall be troubled*
> *And the mountains shall be removed into the*
> *heart of the sea.*

Our days were structured by prayer, teaching, and manual chores. There was no time to indulge our personal taste for literature or music. We didn't read newspapers, listen to the radio, or watch television.

At noon recess we went to the chapel for an examination of conscience that focused on the eradication of one particular fault. That exercise was followed by five minutes of oral spiritual reading from the lector of the week. A parishioner, Mrs. Yeager, prepared the noon meal and washed the dishes so that we could return to school and supervise the children's noon recess.

At four o'clock we took tea in the dining room before Vespers and Compline. From five to six we corrected student papers and prepared our class work. At six o'clock we returned to the chapel for Matins and Lauds.

During supper at six thirty, we passed a book of the lives of the saints and took turns reading aloud. In the kitchen as we washed the dishes and replaced them on the dining table, Mother Inez Pauline stood on the threshold between the two rooms, intoning the short prayers. "Sacred Heart of Jesus…" We answered, "…have mercy on us." Then we went to the community room for recreation. Sitting at the long conference table in order of seniority, we did our mending as we talked. The conversation centered around the events of the day—mostly about school, since we had no other avenues of interest to speak of. At ten minutes to eight, recreation ended and we listened to spiritual reading while we continued with our darning and sewing. At eight o'clock we returned to the chapel for night prayers, after which began "The Grand Silence" and then we retired to our rooms.

On Saturday afternoons I accompanied Sister Jeannette Marie to the church sacristy, where we laid out the priests' vestments for Sunday Mass. We cleaned the sanctuary, put fresh linens on the altar, and set out new candles. Sister Jeannette Marie was older. She had been a staff nurse at a Boston hospital before entering, and for years she'd cared for the elderly infirm nuns at our retirement home in Fall River. That year, with no prior experience in teaching, she'd been asked to teach third grade in Mt. Ephraim. It must have been a difficult transition, but she embraced her assignment with enthusiasm. I liked Sister Jeannette Marie. She was cheerful and kind. Sometimes when we were arranging flowers or working in the sacristy, she would hint at some aspect of Mother's behavior, and it seemed she was just waiting to hear what I had to say. I longed to confide in her, but I'd observed Sister Jeannette Marie's coquettish behavior with Mother and I was afraid she would betray me.

In November my parents made the long trip from Providence—six and a half hours by car. I had not seen them since Profession Day on August twenty-second.

In the parlor my father looked into my eyes.

"Are you happy, sweetheart?"

"Oh, yes, Dad," I lied.

ARTICLE…of the Constitutions: "They are expressly forbidden to impart their troubles or to make the least confidence to anyone whatever from without…"

We'd had to memorize this rule in the novitiate and recite it verbatim like catechism. In addition the novice mistress cautioned us further. "Don't tell your family anything about your life in the convent. They are seculars. They don't understand the religious life, and they can't help you."

I remembered my father's words to me several years before on the day that I entered the convent: "Sweetheart, if you're not happy you always have a place to come home to."

I knew in my heart that my father would not have hesitated to take me away from Mt. Ephraim that day. All I had to do was say the word. And I was tempted to run out and get in the car. Instead I kept up the deception. I was mindful that now I was a vowed religious. If I left without obtaining a dispensation, I would be an apostate nun.

An apostate! It was unthinkable. I would be excommunicated from the Church. In the novitiate Mother Consolata had told us stories of nuns who'd forsaken their religious communities and then denigrated sacred objects and stomped on crucifixes.

No, I couldn't succumb to the temptation to flee.

Besides, I thought of my fourth-graders and what would happen to them if I left. I'd wait until August and then I'd simply not renew my temporary vows.

Sister Maria Gregory wheeled in a cart laden with platters of roast chicken and vegetables for my parents. As impressed as they were by the convent hospitality, my father still couldn't understand the value of a rule that precluded his daughter from sharing the meal with family.

How painful it was for me to sit there while my parents ate dinner, trying to act as if everything was fine.

"Your superior?"

"Oh, yes, she's very kind."

Just before Christmas the Parent-Teacher Organization gave the convent a set of fine china—thin white porcelain plates and teacups edged in silver. After the dishes were uncrated and laid out on the dining table, we stood gazing at them. They looked so fragile that a sneeze might shatter them. I wondered how this luxury fit in with voluntary poverty. From some of the other sisters, I heard oohs and ahs and "Oh, Mother, they're beautiful…"

Mother Inez Pauline's face was glowing as she explained that these were special dishes to be used on feast days. "And don't anyone dare to break one!" she said.

The new china was destined for its first use on Christmas Day, and the table was laden with a white damask linen cloth. Wreaths of holly berries and candles adorned the centerpiece, and chocolates had been placed on each sister's saucer. Because Christmas was a major feast day, we were allowed to talk at meals.

At dinner the mood was more relaxed than usual without the mandatory silence or spiritual reading. We indulged in roast turkey, dressing, mashed potatoes and gravy. Even Mother Inez Pauline seemed to be in a good mood.

When the meal ended we said grace and cleared the table. As usual we did the wash-up in the kitchen. Mother stood in the doorway, watching us without seeming to look at us and leading the short prayers. "Sacred Heart of Jesus," she intoned and we answered, "…have mercy on us."

Several of us stood by the sink as Sister Mary Joseph (yes, I was Marion Joseph and we had a Mary Joseph, too) washed the prized plates. Most of us were probably thinking the same thing, "Don't anyone dare to break one." We kept drying the dishes, saying the prayers. Have mercy. (Yes, please help us not to break anything.) And then the inevitable happened. With the suds still clinging to her fingertips, Sister Mary Joseph remained motionless as the teacup she'd been holding slid to the floor and detached itself from its handle.

Mother stopped the prayers. Sister Mary Joseph began to sob. All of us stood there too numb to move. It was like the "freeze" game that children play where everyone stops on command. Except it wasn't a game. Mother stomped out of the kitchen. I heard the sound of her heavy footfalls on the staircase as she clomped up to her room. Seconds later her door slammed shut. I prayed that she would stay there for the day.

Then a chorus of voices: "Oh, poor Mother. I hope she'll come down. Won't it be awful if she doesn't spend the afternoon with us?" I thought, no, it'll be a gift.

A few days later Mother stopped me outside the refectory. "There is a box addressed to you at the railroad depot. Why did your parents send a package by railroad express that has to be picked up? Now poor Jean will have to drive there to get it."

One evening when all the sisters were at recreation, Mother called me to her room. My eye caught sight of the box on the floor. It was long, about the size of a commercial tomato box. I recognized my mother's handwriting. "Sister, I want you to take this package to the cellar and open it. Then bring it to me."

I thought of Mom and Dad, and the effort they'd put into wrapping the Christmas presents and sending them from Providence. They must have anticipated my pleasure in opening them. And now I was being ordered to open the box by myself in the cellar. I hesitated. "Mother," I said, "would it be all right if I opened this in the community room with the other sisters?"

"IN THE CELLAR!"

"Yes, Mother."

Why? Why was I told to open the presents by my-self in the cellar? Was it because the package came after Christmas? Or because Jean was inconvenienced? Was I being punished for these things over which I had no control? But it was unthinkable to question the motives of my superior.

I felt no joy as I descended the cellar stairs to unwrap the parcel. I tore off the brown wrapping paper and lifted the box's cover. I ripped off the Santa Claus paper from boxes of Colgate toothpaste, Yardley's soap, a tin of fruit-cake, and sewing sundries. I wanted it to be over with.

We didn't keep presents for ourselves. Whenever we received gifts or money, we handed them in. The religious life was a communal life. Our basic needs of food, shelter, and clothing were provided for, but the spirit of poverty precluded keeping superfluities.

In keeping with the rule, I was obliged to show the gifts to Mother, and I remember that, at the time that I presented the box to her, she seemed to have undergone a change of affect. As I entered her room she looked up and smiled. Then before setting the contents aside, she removed a small sewing kit and gave it to me.

I observed Mother Inez Pauline's interactions with parishioners and with the church's pastor. Frequently she mocked parishioners who were some of our most gener-ous benefactors. From time to time a Mrs. Spinelli brought homemade spaghetti and meatballs to the convent. In her falsetto voice, Mother thanked the woman for thinking of us. "So good of you, Mrs. Spinelli."

In private Mother mimicked Mrs. Spinelli's speech. *"Spaghettis, Reverent Mother. I brought the spaghettis.* Spaghettis! HA HA!"

Another parishioner, Mrs. Brophy, the president of the PTO, helped with school fund-raising and did many favors for the convent. Mother referred to her as "B52."

Even the pastor, Father Spezzaferro, was not spared. Father Spezzaferro was a throwback to an earlier time. He dressed in a cassock, never a suit. Middle-aged, short, and round, he walked with a stoop. I pictured him in a little Italian town, tipping his biretta to the women there in the same way he bowed to Mother and the sisters.

Whenever Father Spezzaferro came to the convent to visit, Mother would ask in the sweetest voice, "Father, may we have your blessing, please?"

Then we'd kneel down while Father made the sign of the cross in midair and said, "In nomine patris et filii…" After he left Mother would mimic his bent posture and imitate his peculiar speech: "Good afta noon, Sistas."

Mother ridiculed the children in our charge as well. At night recreation she would invariably have a story about some student's escapades at school. I remember that one of her eighth-grade students was a frequent target. He was referred to as "Jam Coker." Apparently when he was a first-grader and learning to write his name, he had written James as Jam, and the name stuck. "Ha, ha," Mother would say, "you'll never guess what Jam Coker did today."

On one occasion my stockings had not dried by evening so I hung them by the furnace in the main house. The next morning I rose at the first sound of the bell and dressed quickly. I crossed the yard to the main house and hurried to the cellar to find my dry stockings. I pulled them on and fastened them to my garter belt (no pantyhose in those days). Then I realized I'd forgotten to take my shoes along, but I didn't dare go back to the annex for fear of being late. In an effort to camouflage my slippered feet, I yanked down the long skirt of my habit. At the threshold of the chapel, I took a deep breath. Stepping into the aisle I tried to act nonchalant. But as soon as I was abreast of Mother's prie-dieu, she pulled on my veil. "Where are your shoes?" I could hardly believe that, in the dim light, Mother would notice that I was wearing slippers. Maybe she thought I was crazy.

Occasionally Mother would announce a picnic for supper. A picnic meant that we would have sandwiches or subs in the refectory. For dessert we made s'mores— Hershey bars melted on graham crackers, topped with marshmallow fluff. The rule of silence was suspended. Usually when we had a picnic, we would see a movie afterward. We arranged the dining room chairs to vantage point, and Sister Francine set the reel-to-reel projector on a small table facing the portable screen.

During one of the films, *On the Waterfront,* I didn't realize what propelled Mother Inez Pauline to thrust herself in front of the screen to block out a frame. Later on I saw the film again and realized it was the scene where Marlon Brando (Terry) goes to find Eva Marie Saint (Edie). When Terry arrives at Edie's apartment, she is dressed in her slip. Mother must have considered a woman in a slip too scandalous.

On another occasion we saw *The Caine Mutiny*. As the film rolled, two projectors were running simultaneously— one on the screen and one inside my head. I was absorbed by the paranoid captain's bizarre behavior and by the parallels I recognized in my superior. The perfectionism of Captain Queeg, his obsession with detail, his hysterical outbursts, and his punishing of crewmembers for minor infractions—these were mirror reflections of Mother Inez Pauline.

Some days later Mother ordered us to the dining room. I trembled, wondering what was coming. She had Sister Irene bring in a container of strawberries from the refrigerator and place it on the table.

"Some one of you has been taking strawberries out of the container, and I will find out who it is."

And just like Captain Queeg, she began to measure out the number of cups. It was eerie. I wondered if, after seeing the film, she dreamed that one of us had stolen the strawberries. No one admitted to having taken them, and in the end I don't recall anything other than Mother's black mood.

Then there was the cake. My father made a long distance phone call to a local bakery and ordered a decorated cake sent to the convent. When the cake was delivered to the door, Mother opened it in front of me and the other sisters.

"This will go in the freezer," she said.

I pictured my father, smiling at the thought of surprising us. I felt tears coming, but tried not to show how much it hurt.

I didn't realize that Mother's ill treatment of me was an abuse of power. I didn't know how to separate my superior's unhealthy mental state from what I perceived as my obligation to submit my will. I was trying to live up to the ideals that I'd learned in the novitiate and I thought I had to obey without question and suffer my superior's indignities. The saints suffered. Why should I be any different? Besides, Mother Consolata had taught us that God sent suffering to purify us. She quoted St. Teresa of Avila speaking to God: "If this is how you treat your friends, no wonder you have so few."

On Friday afternoons the student body assembled for movies. There were usually two or three eighth-grade boys remanded to the back of the gymnasium for punishment. Their sentence was to kneel facing the wall for the two hours or so while the movie played. Jam Coker was a regular there. At dismissal time the boys would be released from their prison status. Later Mother would gloat over how they'd been punished for their misdeeds. I wish, for the sake of those boys, that I'd reported it to a higher authority, but I'd become so accustomed to abnormal treatment, myself, that it didn't occur to me to do anything about it.

There was an article in the Constitutions of our Congregation that provided for an appeal to a higher superior. I may even have considered this option and then decided not to go through with it, for fear of reprisal. I had no stamps or money to send a letter, and a phone call might have been overheard.

At night I cried myself to sleep. In the day I prayed. I thought of returning to New England in June where I would see my novice mistress and the Provincial. They were holy women. I had so wanted to be a good religious like them. But I could not see myself living the rest of my life in a tortured state.

Around the middle of March, Mother summoned me to her room. I knew from Sister Maria Gregory that this conference was about renewing my vows in August, but I had already decided my future—one that I determined not to share with my superior. Mother Inez Pauline had not earned the privilege of hearing my heart's secrets. As I ascended the stairs, my heart began to palpitate as it did every Sunday morning when I had to face Mother for my weekly conference. I took a deep breath and crossed the threshold. I responded to the dreaded stimulus of her imagined towering presence by regressing to the state of an adolescent. Now I felt even more ill at ease than usual because of the charade I was about to play. I worried that she might detect a tone of falsity in me that would betray my words. The duality of answering her questions about renewal while, at the same time, knowing that I was about to act out a lie created a tension within me.

She was perched on the swivel chair behind her executive desk. I stood facing her. Whatever nervous mannerisms I probably displayed, I cannot recall.

She began: "Sister, you know it's time for you to write your letter to Reverend Mother for your renewal of vows."

"Yes, Mother." *(I'm not telling you, but I have no intention of renewing.)*

"You know that you have had some problems with obedience."

"Yes, Mother." (*How could I obey when you put obstacles in my way?*)

"I don't understand you. You're unconscious."

"Yes, Mother." *Maybe, but I've observed more than you know.*

She rotated on the swivel, eyeing me coolly. I wondered if she'd not been fooled by my subterfuge. All the time she was talking, it occurred to me that she might envy my position. My temporary vows would expire in August, and I had the option of renewing or not. Mother Inez Pauline was at least twice my age. Maybe she would have liked to trade places with me.

My Dual Life

Following that interview with Mother Inez Pauline in March, I lived in the community on two planes. Outwardly I observed all the rubrics of daily life and prayer. I continued to do my cellar function—washing, hanging, and folding clothes. I took my turn preparing breakfast and so on. But inwardly I disengaged myself from the life of the other sisters. I had a secret—a secret that made my encounters with my superior slightly less intolerable. I ignored her barbs, her sarcasm—fortified with the knowledge that her dominion over me would be short-lived. My decision to leave the Congregation at the expiration of vows in August helped put things in perspective. If I could just hold on, I thought, until school closed, I would go to the motherhouse for summer studies, where I would disclose my intention to Reverend Mother.

At the motherhouse in Fall River, the atmosphere was markedly different from that of the Mt. Ephraim Convent. The familiar surroundings of St. Helena's—the twisted wisteria vines that climbed the trellises of the wide veranda; the undulating grassy banks that informed the yard below; the interior of the convent with its chapel of blonde wooden benches; the refectory with oilcloth-covered tables; the long, empty corridors—presented a quasi-monastic ambience. And even though I'd resolved to leave the Congregation in August, I found peace in the simplicity there, and I relished the routine of daily meditation, Mass, the chanting of the Office. It was a joy to be reunited with the sisters of my set. Mornings we took classes and afternoons we were free for study. At noon recreation we sat on the shaded veranda in an assortment of wicker and Adirondack chairs, recounting our teaching experiences. We laughed at each other's funny stories. The climate of love and kindness was a welcome change from the tempestuous year that I'd spent in Mt. Ephraim.

How would I approach Reverend Mother, I wondered—she who had been a spiritual grandmother in my postulant days and a support to me through the novitiate. I recalled how sometimes after I'd finished mopping and dusting on the second floor of St. Helena's, I'd pass by her office. The door was usually open, but I'd knock. Reverend Mother would look up from her desk and give me a broad smile.

"Come in, Marion," she'd say, inviting me to sit next to her. Pushing aside a pile of papers, she'd give me her undivided attention as if I were the only sister in the province. When I expressed doubts about my vocation. she'd listen to me and give me assurance that I was where God wanted me to be.

But now I was not convinced that this was the life for me. I didn't want to hear from the lips of Reverend Mother: "This is where God wants you to be."

The cruelty, the lack of respect exhibited by my superior—not only toward myself, but toward the parishioners, the children, and even the priests—sickened me. This was not where I wanted to be.

Yet somehow in the midst of taking classes at the Normal School and reuniting with so many of the young sisters, I felt myself being drawn in again. We shared an affection, a camaraderie for each other. Maybe it was something akin to American soldiers volunteering for multiple tours to stay connected with their buddies.

Also there was an air of otherworldliness at St. Helena's. It was monastic down to the oilcloth-covered refectory tables. There were no bibelots. Everyone was in earnest about a spiritual life. At our recreations we laughed a lot but never at anyone's expense.

I was aware of a gradual interior change taking place in me. I experienced peace and I felt a longing to recover the fervor that had been mine. Perhaps it was self-hypnosis, but I turned more to contemplation and reconsidered the taking of vows.

By the time I had my heart-to-heart with Reverend Mother, I was resolute in my decision to renew my vows. But I asked her not to send me back to Mt. Ephraim—this in direct contradiction to the rule that stated the sisters would go willingly to the places they were sent. Without recounting all of the abuses, I indicated to her that I could not go back to live under my former superior. (I learned later that someone else in the community had given Reverend Mother an earful.)

As always she listened to me. "Don't worry, Sister. I can't say too much now, but I promise you this: You'll not have the same situation again. Following your retreat I'll be sending you to St. Peter's in Point Pleasant. You'll stay there until you hear from me."

I trusted her and I inferred from her remarks that I'd be returning to Mt. Ephraim with a different superior. The summer passed quickly, with final exams ending our college courses. And then it was time for retreat.

Eight days of silence and prayer In the chapel listening to the homilies of the Jesuit retreat master. I went deeply into the retreat, immersing myself in contemplation and spiritual reading. Walking about in the garden with eyes cast down, yet somewhat aware of other black-clad forms moving along the path, I knew my sisters were engaged in their own renewal. I was not alone.

On the last day of retreat, I would consecrate myself to my heavenly Bridegroom. A spark had been rekindled in me. In the Canticle of Canticles, I found the poetry that ignited my soul:

Let Him kiss me with the kiss of His mouth
O Thou whom my soul loves…
A bundle of myrrh is my Beloved to me. He shall abide between my two breasts.
Stay me up with flowers, compass me about with apples because I languish withlove.
His left hand is under my head. His right hand shall embrace me.
Behold my Beloved speaks to me: Arise, my love. My dove, my beautiful one
And come.

Point Pleasant Interlude

When I arrived at St. Peter's, only two sisters were there—the rest not yet back from retreat. I spent my time praying and reading while anticipating a phone call or letter from Reverend Mother.

Point Pleasant was, *is*, a town on the Jersey Shore, and though not so monumental a place as Atlantic City or Asbury Park, there was a beach I could have gone to. But it never occurred to me to do so without permission.

Each night I placed my thin black rulebook under my pillow before going to sleep. It gave me comfort. Now as I consider this, I marvel at how I could have derived comfort from the harsh and outmoded injunctions contained in the Holy Rule. But I think I was nostalgic for the connection to the familiar at Rock Street.

One day a sister returning to Point Pleasant from Fall River handed me an envelope written in Mother Gabriel Clare's hand. I opened it and removed the letter, which I read three times. Reverend Mother's words were reassuring: "Sister, a new superior awaits you in Mt. Ephraim."

She wished me well and gave me her blessing. So that was it. I was going back to Mt. Ephraim.

Mt. Ephraim Revisited

Mother Mary Kieran, the new superior, was already installed at the Mt. Ephraim convent when I arrived from Point Pleasant. She was energetic and appeared to be in her mid-thirties. She talked and laughed, sometimes making jokes. Was this free style of hers temporary, I wondered. She seemed too modern for my image of *mother superior*. But maybe she had to relax the rule a bit while she got her bearings in the community and the school. As superior *cum* principal she'd have a lot of responsibility, and in addition she would teach one of the two eighth-grade classes. There was flurry and excitement as all of us bustled back and forth from convent to school, working in our classrooms, writing lesson plans, and preparing for the students. Mother Mary Kieran distributed copious sheets of schedules—timetables, recess duty, and dismissal procedures.

Lists of functions appeared on the bulletin board of the

community room. There were lists for making breakfast and supper, lists for wash-up, lists for reading at the table, lists for the weekly presider for chanting the Office, and so on.

Mother Mary Kieran was the epitome of efficiency. And she took an interest in household décor—table-settings, dishes, upholstery, etc. One of her innovations was the ordering of new draperies for the community room. The draperies were no sooner delivered than she opened the package herself and stood on a stepstool to hang them. I couldn't muster much enthusiasm for the beige drapes embossed with white camellias. I questioned why we needed them. We were vowed to a life of poverty and simplicity. What about that? I longed for the Spartan furnishings of Rock Street.

Mother Mary Kieran's *cause célébre* was obedience. Not long after she was in command, she mounted a sign above the holy water font at the chapel's entry:

If you need to use your handkerchief, please leave the chapel.

In the chapel our places were assigned in order of seniority. We sat at prie-dieux, arranged in sets of twos. Unlike a church pew the prie-dieu is a kneeler with a chair attached. In ranking order, Sister Albertine and I sat up front, and both of us suffered from seasonal allergies and rhinitis. In order to comply with obedience, we alternately left the chapel during spiritual exercises.

Sitting quietly at morning meditation, suddenly I'd get a fit of sneezing, genuflect, and exit the chapel like an exile leaving her country.

On re-entry I'd genuflect again and take my seat. Typically several minutes would elapse before—ka-CHOO! Sister Albertine, sitting next to me and straining to stifle her sneezes, would get up, climb over me and my kneeler, genuflect, and hurry out of the chapel. Seconds later she was back, genuflecting in the aisle and clambering over my feet. It was a parade, particularly in allergy season, and I often wondered if our constant bobbing up and down was not a greater distraction to those sitting behind us than an auditory assault would have been, had we remained seated.

On one occasion when my rhinitis was exacerbated by a head cold, I opted for common sense. Surely the rule didn't apply in such a circumstance. I remained in my seat, blowing into my handkerchief.

Suddenly Mother Mary Kieran was standing in the aisle, motioning me out of the chapel. She pushed me in front of the sign above the holy water font.

"Can you read?"

"Yes, Mother. I…I have a cold. I thought…"

"No exceptions. Do you understand?"

"Yes, Mother."

I wanted to understand Mother Mary Kieran. She

seemed pragmatic. Endless lists of regulations and enforcement of strict obedience. Yet she appeared dismissive of the rule of silence. There was, however, none of the unpredictability that had existed under Mother Inez Pauline, and that was something to be thankful for. No, Mother Mary Kieran was not crazy and she was not sadistic. You knew where you stood with her.

But she was tough on obedience. I remember one time that she scolded me for "failing in obedience" when I arrived to school ten minutes late for prep time. Mass that morning had been delayed and I needed to hang the wash outside. (At least Mother Mary Kieran didn't make me take the clothesline in every night.) As I was pegging the undergarments to the line, I checked my watch. Realizing I was already late I kept on until the last towel was hung.

I crossed the yard and entered the school building. She was waiting for me. "You're very late," she said.

"Yes, Mother. Sorry. I saw that I was late and so I decided to finish hanging."

"You mean you thought you might as well hang for a sheep as for a lamb."

"I guess something like that, Mother."

"Well, it's a failure in obedience."

"Yes, Mother," I said. But I wondered how I could square obeying the school rule and fulfilling my assigned duty.

Sister Margaret Lucy's habit of mocking me in front

of the community went unchecked because of the high school friendship between her and my superior. At recreation Sister Margaret Lucy would embarrass me with little anecdotes about my failures. The sisters would laugh, but to me her remarks were harpoons.

I was learning about human nature—not from books but from the sisters I observed. The community was a microcosm of the world outside—human beings with all the attendant virtues and vices that exist everywhere.

I was beginning to realize that the world of the novitiate and the world of mission were very different. The novitiate had been a hothouse of spirituality and idealism where everyone was striving for perfection. We were all teenagers full of fervor.

In the world of the active apostolate, we were a community of mixed ages. The most senior sister was in her early sixties. Another was about fifty, the rest—in their thirties or forties. Only two of us were younger.

Generally the early years of life are the most optimistic. After time ennui sets in, and it is much harder to maintain the enthusiasm of youth. Then there are personal dynamics—a person's childhood, upbringing, family values, character traits, etc.

Mt. Ephraim was miles away from the motherhouse and miles away from influence. It was harder to remain true to the spirit of the Congregation when separated from the roots. But also I think that for those who had been religious for a long time, there really wasn't a lot to look forward to. The life was repetitious and imposed restraint. Yet I couldn't excuse certain behaviors like Sister Margaret Lucy's.

Sister Margaret Lucy came to recreation one night holding aloft a ravaged shirtwaist. "Look what I found under a pile of leaves," she said.

I took it in at a glance—the dirty shirtwaist torn and full of holes—and I knew it was Sister Margaret Lucy at it again. I was the cellarer. The laundry was my responsibility. All eyes were on me. Then Sister Margaret Lucy put her hand to her mouth. "Oh, I'm sorry. I didn't mean to get you in trouble."

I should have defended myself, but I was too intimidated, and that probably made the game more enjoyable for her. Offering up little slights is one of the things St. Therese did, but it was bad advice.

At the end of the year we closed school and dispersed for college courses and retreat.

I returned in August to begin my third year in Mt. Ephraim—still assigned to teach fourth grade. There were a few transfers—Sister Margaret Lucy not among them—and Mother Mary Kieran in charge.

Early in October something happened that caused a chain of events. Some of the children subscribed to a weekly Catholic magazine that, I think, was called *The*

Junior Catholic Messenger. It featured articles on the life of Jesus, church history, and games with kid appeal. One of the issues focused on Our Lady of the Rosary, the special feast day, October 7. A particular article spoke of dedication to Mary through prayers and devotions. There was a "how to" section on crafting religious artifacts from crepe paper, cardboard, and aluminum foil that might be carried in procession to honor Mary.

The children brought in materials and, following the instructions in the periodical, we fashioned aluminum-covered "knights' swords" for the boys, capes and sashes for the girls. We planned a procession to the church, where we would kneel at the communion rail and recite our Consecration to Mary.

The children were lined up two by two, and the procession made its way across the schoolyard. Slowly, solemnly, we entered the nave of the church and made our way down the aisle. After genuflecting we knelt at the communion rail. Then in unison everyone read the prayer of Consecration to Mary.

No one had been in the church when we entered. But just as we were ready to leave, the pastor appeared. "Good afta noon, Sista."

That was how it sounded when Father Spezzafera spoke.

"Good afternoon, Father," I said.

"What is this, Sista?" he asked.

I explained.

He scratched his head and went away.

After school dismissal, Mother Mary Kieran sent for me. What was the idea of dressing the children up with swords and taking them to the church without permission? It hadn't occurred to me to ask permission. I thought what I'd done was in consonance with teaching religion. Well, it wasn't according to Mother Mary Kieran. And the pastor had come to inquire. By evening all the sisters knew about the unorthodox pilgrimage and the spectacle I'd made.

Sister Margaret Lucy, with her penchant for *schadenfreude*, probably fed off that for a week. I'm sure it was she who started the rumor that I'd had a nervous breakdown.

About a week after the "procession," Mother Mary Kieran sent me to a doctor in Haddonfield, a town near Mt. Ephraim. She didn't give a reason for the visit, and I was puzzled. Sister Albertine accompanied me—even to the examining room. The doctor was pleasant enough, and the exam was the most comprehensive physical I ever had, before or since. He examined my limbs. He had me stretch out my legs at right angles. Then, the stethoscope, ophthalmoscope, and blood pressure monitor. He even had me look at reading charts to determine my visual acuity.

When he concluded he said he was giving me two prescriptions:

One was a prescription for corrective lenses. (He said I had compound myopic astigmatism.) And the second, a prescription for vitamins. I wondered why I'd need a prescription for vitamins when they could be bought over the counter.

At the convent Mother Mary Kieran took the paperwork from Sister Albertine. I must have gone to an optician, though I cannot remember doing so. But I did get glasses that I began to wear all the time. As for the vitamin prescription—it turned out to be a bottle of capsules containing little green and white granules that I was to take once a day. Once on the regimen, I began to feel euphoric. I was practically flying. What I know now and did not know then is that these *vitamins* were probably amphetamines like Dexedrine—popular in the late fifties and early sixties. I was taking uppers! But why did the good doctor lie to me? Why the deception?

Soon after the doctor visit, Mother Mary Kieran told me that Reverend Mother had asked me to the motherhouse. I had no idea why she wanted to see me, but I was glad to go to Fall River.

On my arrival at the Provincial House, Reverend Mother Gabriel Clare seemed pleased to see me. We sat at the rolltop desk in the sparsely furnished room that was her office.

"Marion," she said, "I'm sending you to St. William's in Baltimore. Mother Agatha, the superior of St. William's, is here and you'll go down with her on the train. I think the change will be good for you."

I accepted this bit of news without a qualm. "Thank you, Reverend Mother," I said. "I think I'll like that."

The Transfer to St. William's

In Providence, at Union Station, Mother Agatha and I boarded the train for Baltimore. When at last we were seated in the coach section, she said:

"You have no idea how sad I am to be losing Sister William Therese. Such a good sister! So devoted."

"Yes, I'm sorry," I said.

I waited for some words of assurance from her, some encouragement as I embarked on my new assignment. But there were no kind words—nothing from her that indicated a warm welcome. I had the aisle seat, and as the train hur tled along the tracks through Westerly and the seemingly endless miles of roadbed into Connecticut, Mother Agatha kept up the lamentation. I looked past her and gazed out the window, hoping for a distraction.

It was like a wake. I shrank down in my seat, feeling impoverished for what I had to offer. I wondered how I could live up to the model behavior of Sister William Therese, so beloved by Mother Agatha. Maybe, I thought, I might have been better off staying in the New Jersey convent. Reverend Mother Gabriel Clare had been so maternal, so supportive and caring—the way she'd always been with me since my days as a postulant. I assumed her best intentions in sending me to St William's. She could not have known what a cruel joke it was turning out to be.

The train ride was long. In New Haven we had a layover while the engineers changed to a different track gauge and more travelers got on.

"Tickets, please," said the conductor. These were the last words I heard. When I woke up we were in Baltimore.

At the convent Mother Agatha convened the community. Most of the sisters were young, and many of them were my peers from the novitiate. As they gathered around they welcomed me warmly. Mother singled out Sister William Therese and said,

"I have something here that will make you want to throw up."

She handed her a small white envelope. Sister William Therese's face betrayed no emotion as she slit the envelope open and read the card indicating her reassignment to Mt. Ephraim.

The reason for the exchange was not clear to me. Normally transfers were given in August before the start of the school year. Now it was October, and classes had been in operation for several weeks.

Sister William Therese was probably feeling sad at being uprooted from a place that she liked, but she appeared serene and displayed no resentment toward me.

I had known her briefly from the time I entered at the Sacred Hearts Convent in Fall River. She was a senior novice then and was sent out on mission before we made the move to Rock Street. I remembered her as a novice, a model of method and perfection who seemed to do everything right. How would I be able to replace her?

After breakfast on the following day, Sister William Therese took me to the school adjacent to the convent. A locked door led through to a corridor from which all the classrooms opened on one floor. We entered the first-grade room where I would be teaching the next day. Sister William Therese's plan book lay open on her desk with a week's worth of activities. She showed me her manuals for reading, phonics, and math and explained the three groupings for reading: the Lilliputian chairs where one group at a time would come up to read in the front of the room.

I was impressed by the way Sister William Therese had orchestrated her classroom. This was probably only her fifth year of teaching, but she had mastered her craft. As a perfectionist she'd always been chosen to iron the guimpes and "do the bands." Yet she was humble and she was kind. A person so quiet you would almost forget she was there.

The next day I greeted the first-graders. After teaching fourth-grade students, these children appeared so small.

I don't remember if Mother Agatha introduced me or if I did it myself. When the thirty or so children came into the classroom, they asked: "Where is Sister William Therese?"

I had interrupted their routine, their structure. It took a few days for them and for me to accommodate. The children seemed very bright and eager to learn. This was an upper-middle-class parish, and most of the parents were college graduates. One boy, William, was as tall as a fourth-grader and already reading on an advanced level.

It was very different teaching six-year-olds. But as time went on, I loved seeing their progress. How excited they were to write and to understand words in print. I enjoyed their spontaneity and I was in awe of their innocence. Once when I was supervising the children who stayed for lunch, a boy named John Cahill said wistfully, "My mother gives me grizzle sandwiches."

Because the school had a larger enrollment at that level, we had two first-grade classes on shifts. Sister Kathleen Joseph taught the morning shift, and I—the afternoon class. My schedule was noon to four thirty. Mornings when everyone else was in school, I did the laundry and prepared my classes.

Often Mother Agatha reprimanded me or compared me to Sister Kathleen Joseph or Sister Nora William, who did things more efficiently than I. Sometimes she told me I didn't show enough initiative. When I assumed more responsibility, she told me I was too independent. Once when I was on yard duty before school, an enormous dog bounded onto the playground and terrified the children. I ran inside and represented the situation to Mother Agatha, asking for the phone directory. I called the dog pound and spoke to the attendant, who assured me he would send someone to the school.

"It's all taken care of, Mother," I said when I handed her the phone book. "They're going to send someone right away."

Steely-eyed she stared at me. "You didn't have permission to call the dog pound. I only gave you the directory."

On Sundays we were obliged to go to Mother's room for our weekly interview and to renew permissions. Her authority cowed me, and whenever I stepped across the threshold, my heart would race. *What will it be today?* I'd wonder. It seemed there was always a cutting remark from her, a sinister laugh. I began to think of Mother Agatha as a fox. She had a way of snarling and showing her teeth that was menacing.

I'd cringe, bracing myself for the plethora of faults she would have observed in me during the week. Fear must have showed on my face. How can one live in such an atmosphere of anxiety without some physical manifestation?

"You don't consult me and ask my advice."

I didn't want to ask Mother Agatha's advice about anything. I avoided her whenever I could. I was inadequate. I bungled everything I did. I was worthless. These were the messages I internalized. Often I was sick with tonsillitis or laryngitis. I'd lose my voice for days, and Sister Mary David had to teach my afternoon class as well as her morning group.

Maybe a more perspicacious superior might have connected my continual bouts of illness and fatigue as symptoms of depression. Instead Mother Agatha, on such occasions, berated me for overburdening Sister Mary David.

"I hope you realize how hard Sister Mary David is working to carry your class. She's in school all day."

Yes, I felt terrible about not being able to teach my class, and I knew it was putting an extra demand on Sister Mary David. Not for the world would I have wished it. I felt guilty enough.

I was mindful that as my superior, Mother Agatha represented the voice of God (strange though it seems, in hindsight, that such an unkind person could be the vehicle for expressing God's will). Because of this belief that had been dinned into me from novitiate days, it never occurred to me to challenge anything Mother Agatha said. I would, instead, acquiesce. Occasionally, in spite of trying not to let her see me cry, I would burst into tears. I felt alone and abandoned, and I reverted to a childish state.

Mother Agatha was my superior during the three years that I was stationed at St. William's, and what had started out badly between us did not get any better. The only thing that made my life in any way supportable was the spirit of love and kindness exemplified by the other sisters in community.

In my last year there, I was still in charge of laundry and I spent solitary mornings in the cellar. Mother Agatha taught the second-grade morning class while Sister Barbara Thomas took music classes at the Peabody Institute. A lay cook came in mid-morning to cook the noon meal, and apart from that there was no one else in the house at that time.

Looking back now it seems incomprehensible that sometime during that third year I contemplated ending my life. I suppose it was a combination of things—my feelings of worthlessness and a sensation of abandonment while I worked alone in the cellar. To kill myself was completely irrational, especially because as a professed nun I believed that suicide was a mortal sin. I was in despair and I considered that to be the only way to end my suffering.

I had thought of a method. It would be gas from the kitchen stove. I would have to do it before Joanne, the cook, came in around ten o'clock. I'd turn on all the jets and in a little while I'd be dead. Joanne would probably be the first to find me lying on the kitchen floor. I didn't consider the sisters' feelings about my act of desperation. I thought about my suicide for days. I cannot say what caused me to abandon the plan. I think I may have considered the possibility of one of the sisters coming in through the connecting door from the school and finding me half unconscious. Or maybe I reasoned that someone else might lose consciousness.

Whatever stopped me, I realized how close I had come to ending it all, and it was a shock even to me that I had contemplated snuffing out my life. I had kept these suicidal thoughts to myself, feeling bereft of anyone to whom I could open my heart. Certainly I would not confide in Mother Agatha. And it didn't occur to me to mention it to my confessor. Ironically the only ones I would have turned to would have been my sisters in community, most of whom I'd known since novitiate days. My choice would have been Sister Kathleen Joseph, but speaking, much less, confiding in anyone was against the Rule.

Gradually, without talking therapy or drugs, I began to heal myself. Maybe I saw, as the end of the school year approached, that I would be going back to the motherhouse in Fall River for summer study. Returning to that milieu with all the young sisters gave me something to look forward to. I'd somehow emerged from the netherworld.

Before Memorial Day Mother Agatha approached me one day and said, "Sister, we're going to have a picnic and entertainment for the St. Edward's sisters on Saturday. I'm putting you in charge of the food."

Mother was giving me this responsibility? She trusted me enough to prepare the food for our guests? I wanted to show her that I could live up to the expectation.

"We'll have cold cuts, rolls, potato salad…"

I was memorizing every item down to the last pickle. It thrilled me to be considered for something so important. I was determined to show Mother Agatha that I was up to the task.

The "picnic" was to be an indoor affair, served in the refectory. Of course the rule of silent eating would be suspended, and the St. Edward's sisters would be our guests at the table.

After Mass that morning I set the table and later I arranged platters of cold cuts, sandwiches, pickles, bowls of potato chips, and the other items on the menu that Mother had ordered. The eight sisters from St. Edward's arrived with Mother Anne Joseph, and we embraced them in our customary style. We knew all the sisters from St. Edward's, and it was thrilling for our two communities to celebrate together.

After everyone had gathered in the refectory, Mother Agatha said Grace and the feast began. I handed Mother a platter of sandwiches, congratulating myself that I'd managed everything so well. Maybe from now on I would be counted among the reliable ones. Mother turned toward me and made her typical grimace, which showed her canine teeth. Narrowing her eyes, she glared at me. "Where's the potato salad?"

"Oh, coming right up, Mother," I said. I'd completely forgotten the potato salad, but I was determined not to let her best me this time. I ran to the cellar and filled my apron with several large potatoes. Returning to the kitchen I grabbed a big pot and filled it with hot water from the tap. I covered the pot and set it over one of the gas burners on the oversized stove, turning the jet up so that the flames licked the sides of the aluminum pot, blackening it all around. While the water boiled I sliced onions and celery. When the potatoes were soft enough, I peeled off their jackets and threw them into a big ceramic dish with the cut-up vegetables and heaps of mayonnaise, some salt and pepper.

Triumphantly, like the Egyptians entering the gate in Verdi's *Aida*, I entered the refectory, holding aloft my dish. "Here you are, Mother," I said, "the potato salad." I could almost hear the strains of that operatic march playing inside my head.

Mother gave me a crafty look, but never mentioned the incident again. It didn't matter. The victory was mine.

There was more to come that day. We had prepared a show to entertain the St. Edward's sisters in the school auditorium. Mother had not seen us rehearse, so it was to be a surprise for her. Someone announced the first act, "Barnyard Serenade," and the curtain went up. Sister Barbara Thomas, with the beautiful voice, bounded onto the stage—her skirts hiked up and a feather duster pinned to her backside. Cackling like a hen, she strutted around in circles like a barnyard chicken. The St. Edward's sisters and Mother Anne Joseph were doubled over, holding their sides.

I watched Mother Agatha's face grow redder and redder until I thought she might have a stroke of apoplexy. Sister Barbara Thomas bowed to an encore.

Next up I was on with Sister Jane Raymond, who suffered from rheumatoid arthritis. Her feet were so disfigured from the disease that walking was an effort. She was such a good sport that we'd gotten the idea to do a kind of pas de deux that we titled "Russian Ballet." We hammed it up to make it comical. And everyone applauded except Mother Agatha.

After our guests left, Mother assembled us in the community room. "I was never so humiliated," she told us. "What you sisters did was a disgrace to Holy Union. I was mortified in front of Mother Anne Joseph. You, Sister Barbara Thomas, why didn't you sing Mozart's 'Magnificat'? We're sending you to Peabody to study music." That was Mother Agatha's parting remark before she stalked off to her room.

Early in June we closed school for the year and went to New England for vacation and study. In August the new provincial superior, Mother Mary William, transferred me to St. Mary's in Taunton.

Mother Agatha asked to speak to me. "I know I've been

hard on you," she said, "but I couldn't help myself. Every time I saw you cross my threshold, you seemed so timid that I…I couldn't help myself. I do the same thing with the second-graders."

St. Mary's, Taunton

Mother Margaret Imelda, my new superior at St Mary's, could have been a stand-in for the abbess in *The Sound of Music*. She had the mien and girth of a prioress, and she was easy to approach. Maybe because of her heart condition (angina) she hadn't the stamina to follow me around and scold me, but I think it was not in her nature to harass anyone. Accustomed as I was to humiliation from my previous superiors, I found it hard to believe that I was respected and treated as an adult.

Mother Margaret Imelda was charged with governing about twenty sisters of mixed ages, some of whom, I gleaned, presented challenges to her. There was the high school faculty of mostly ageing nuns, and the grammar school faculty of nuns younger in age and seniority, as well as a full-time sister-cook.

In nun-speak, a word for *nonconforming* characters was *oiseau*, the French for *bird*. By simple observation of their outward demeanor and by their general noncompliance with the rules, I conjectured that there were one or two *birds* in our convent.

One was Sister Suzanne, a sprightly nun, about fifty, with darting brown eyes. Sister Suzanne practically lived in the linen room and never came to recreation. As linen keeper she was in charge of keeping the nuns' *paquets* of clothes and setting out the Sunday habits once a week. Apart from that she did some mending and, it seemed, endless cutting out of patterns and sewing on the machine. She did her school prep and corrected her seventh-grade student papers there, too. I think she liked working in solitude. Absenting oneself from community recreation was an infraction of the Rule that most superiors would not have tolerated. The Rule stated:

> *"The Religious are always all together for the recreations, except when their duty or obedience keeps them elsewhere, or when the Superior has dispensed them from attendance."*

Sometimes I'd stop by the linen room. "Come in, Marion," Sister Suzanne would say. She was a gentle soul, an astute thinker, and more often than not, critical of the religious life. Though I didn't agree with her assessments about the convent, I enjoyed her company. What was happening to me? I'd been so careful to observe the rule of silence, but now I was allowing myself to engage in conversation.

The high school sisters were past middle age, and I found them to be delightful. I suppose years had made them mellow and somewhat commonsensical about observance of the Rule. Theirs was more the spirit than the letter. Sister Stanislaus Joseph, trig and algebra teacher in the high school, was the convent sacristan. She cared for the priests' linens, set out the vestments for Mass, and decorated the altar with flowers. I offered to be her assistant, and we established good rapport. I was amused by her occasional expressions of frustration when we had all the candles lit for Benediction and then learned that "Father" would be late for the service. "Darn," she'd say.

Sister Michael Joseph, science teacher, approaching ninety years, had come over from Ireland years before, and still spoke with a lilt to her voice. I remember her sitting in the community room reading *The Taunton Gazette.* Tossing the newspaper aside she'd get up out of her chair, flash me an infectious smile, and say, "Kid! I'll be in my lab if anyone's looking for me." She seemed to have the liberty of retreating, at will, to the chemistry annex.

I loved teaching third grade, and my principal, Sister James Alberta, was supportive and open to letting me explore creative ideas and incorporating conceptual approaches like Cuisenaire rods for math.

During that year I was preparing to take perpetual vows

in August, and I had the highest hopes to spend the rest of my life in the Congregation. When school ended in June, I packed my bag and joined the other eight sisters in my set at the motherhouse in Fall River. We were in seclusion there as we entered into a kind of spiritual retreat leading up to the vow ceremony in August.

Our directress was Sister John Alicia, not only a deeply spiritual person, but also someone with a great understanding of human nature. Sister John Alicia had studied literature and drama at Catholic University, and we benefited from her rich experience in theatre arts. In addition to our daily lecture on the spiritual life, we spent our time praying, reading, and reflecting. At noon recreation our little band joined the other young nuns from the summer study group on the veranda of St. Helena's. I was happy in the camaraderie of so many of the sisters I'd known from the novitiate.

On August twenty-second, 1961, along with my peer group of eight sisters, I pronounced my perpetual vows according to the Constitutions of the Congregation of the Religious of the Holy Union.

At St. Mary's, during my first year, I'd been so relieved to be in a supportive community, I think I played the role of "good sister," docile and demure. Now I was breaking free and growing in my own identity. Maybe in that supportive environment, free from fear and constant criticism, my suppressed self reemerged and was further nourished during the summer retreat in preparation for final vows.

As the school year began, a plan got under way to implement physical changes in the Prospect Street Convent. Reverend Mother Mary William was enjoined by new directives coming from the Holy See to modernize living conditions for the sisters. To finance the project she set up a million-dollar funding campaign and proposed that the sisters from all our convents in Fall River and Taunton form a nuns' glee club and orchestra. We had many talented musicians who played instruments and at least three sisters who were professionals.

It meant that many of us would get together on Saturdays to rehearse, usually at Sacred Hearts in Fall River. The orchestra had a large string section, wind and brass, kettledrums and cymbals. Sister Maurice Louise, our resident musician, gave me lessons on the viola. I loved its melancholy sound and I practiced until I could play some simple tunes. I eventually got to play a piece I loved called "The Celtic Lament."

I wasn't able to keep up the pace, though, and finally had to drop out of the orchestra. But I sang alto in the glee club. We sang, In addition to sacred music, popular songs and a piece set to the music of Tchaikovsky, for which Sister Steven Helen brought in a professional choir director to coach us. I remember the orchestra playing a part of *The Jupiter* and also the "Wedding March" from Mendelssohn's *Midsummer Night's Dream*. We took our show on the road, performing in different venues in

Providence, Connecticut, and New York City. Sister James Alberta had a trumpet solo in *Tammy* with glee club and orchestra combined. Our families supported the venture and people loved it. We eventually cut some records and sold them.

At the end of that school year, after promotion lists and records had been sent to the office, Sister James Alberta left the Congregation. She left without saying good-bye. Her chair in the refectory was vacant. And somehow the news filtered down—Sister James Alberta was gone. That was how it was done in those days—in secret. It was rare for a perpetually professed sister to leave the Congregation. It was a shock, and I was saddened.

Sister Suzanne was holding court in the linen room. She looked up as I stood in the doorway. "Come in, Marion," she said in her modulated tone. "What do you think about Sister James Alberta?"

I think she got her answer from the look on my face. I nodded. Sister Mary Charles, one of the older nuns said, "For ten cents I'd do what she did."

And I thought it sad that Sister Mary Charles, probably near to seventy, wished to leave, but for whatever reason was not about to go. It was no secret that Sister Mary Charles was not happy. I felt sorry that she would have no peace.

Prospect Street and Puerto Rico

August 1962

Summer study was over and most of us were assembled in the cobblestoned courtyard of Sacred Hearts Convent, steadying our nerves as we waited out the annual distribution of billets-doux. All eyes were on the cloister door. Presently Reverend Mother Mary William emerged and descended the steps—a stack of white envelopes in her hand. Greeting us with a kindly smile, she said, "Sisters, I hope you will accept any changes as God's will for you."

Then she began calling out names—mine among them. I was transferred to Sacred Hearts Convent (commonly called Prospect Street).

Out loud I said, "But I don't want to leave St. Mary's." I watched some sisters—tears streaming down their faces and others showing a bit of temper. To be uprooted from a beloved community—even if it was the will of God—was no small thing.

Now I would live in this convent that at one time had held such nostalgia for me when I was a boarder in eighth grade.

That was then. Now it was not the same. I was a nun with perpetual vows.

Gone was the look of the original building. Only the mullion-windowed cloister wing remained. With reconstruction, some land had had to be sacrificed (a parcel had been sold to the adjacent Union Hospital), and the main entrance was no longer at the top of Prospect Hill but around the corner in the courtyard.

Behind the heavy glass security doors, there were several small parlors for visitors and a dining room—kept for the priests who came to say Mass. The large airy community room on the first floor was furnished with ten or twelve square tables. The kitchen was equipped with stainless steel sinks, prep tables, and restaurant-sized appliances.

On the second floor the gothic chapel remained, connected by a corridor to the high school classrooms. In the cloistered section, instead of a dormitory with curtained partitions, each sister now had a private room furnished with a bed, an armoire, a desk, and a sink—complete with mirror. Casement windows accorded light and brought in views of the garden to the rear and the courtyard in the front.

I'd often thought of the older sisters in the dormitory—no privacy, enduring sounds of snoring and coughing night after night. It must have been irksome and impossible to sleep—particularly for those with infirmities. Now after all these years, the old thin mattresses on the wooden planks had been replaced with comfortable bedding.

I knew many of the sisters in the community—some from my days at boarding school and others whom I'd met at our summer residence. The Prospect Street Convent comprised forty to forty-five sisters staffing the high school academy, the elementary academy, and the two parochial schools—Holy Name and St. Michael's. This was a community of women of diverse ages and temperaments. Maybe the sheer size of the physical building contributed to a feeling of depersonalization or maybe it was that we taught in different schools—but we did not seem to be a cohesive community. There was no real sense of belonging. A subtle sense of hierarchy was present amongst us—with the staffs of the high school academy in the upper echelon, followed in descending order by the elementary academy and the three parish schools. Many of the older sisters retired to their rooms immediately after supper while the rest of us took recreation in the community room, playing Scrabble or bid whist.

On Saturday mornings a small group of us went off in a VW van to Providence, where we attended classes at La Salle Academy under the auspices of Catholic Teachers' College—accredited to grant baccalaureate degrees. We needed to supplement our normal school credits to complete our degrees.

The three-hour classes at La Salle and the round trip from Fall River consumed half a day. On return we ate lunch and began our housekeeping responsibilities. Saturday was the day for big cleaning. Floors were scrubbed, waxed, and polished. In the chapel pews were dusted and aisles swept. In the dining room tables and chairs were moved and dusted. There were a lot of rooms to clean, and since a great number of the sisters were older, the responsibility fell to us younger ones.

I was assigned to teach fifth grade at St. Michael's, where most of the students were first generation, born of immigrant parents (many from the Azores), and I was introduced to a language and culture that I found exotic. There were saints' feasts—and food was a big part of the celebration. In the church hall platters were piled high with *chouriço* and *linguiça*, breads and *malasadas* (fried dough) and cookies.

For the feast of the Holy Ghost (Pentecost), a lively procession marched through the streets—one of the most colorful parades I'd ever seen. Tubas, trombones, horns, and drums called everyone to join in. Elaborately constructed floats decorated with the colors of the Portuguese flag moved past St. Michael's Church. A dove representing the Holy Ghost was held aloft for all to see. The dove appeared alive enough to fly out of the hand that held it, but instead the paper bird was carried to the home of a chosen family, where it would remain for a day and be alternately passed on to other host families during the octave of the feast.

Rituals such as this, carried over from Portugal and the islands, provided the new arrivals a link to their homeland as they transitioned to a culture so different from their own. The hope was for the children to learn the language and customs of the new country while retaining respect for their heritage.

The students were at an age where their thinking was more abstract. I loved the kids. I found them to be respectful for the most part—except when there were playground fights.

Once when I tried to intervene in a gang fight, I was accidentally knocked down and landed on the bottom of the heap. One of the sisters helped me to my feet.

"Don't get into their scuffles," she said. "These kids are hoods!"

I heard some of the boys saying FUCK. I didn't even know what the word meant, but only that it was *bad*. I spoke to Father Oliveira. "Father," I said, "would you have a talk with the boys about their language?" I didn't dare to articulate the word, so I spelled it. "Father, they are saying, F-U-C-K."

"Sure, Sister, I'll speak to them."

Oh, what a good laugh those priests must have had when Father Oliveira told them, at supper that night, what the good sister had said.

Of my teaching assignments I enjoyed St. Michael's more than any other. I think it was partly because I was more involved in the parish celebrations and got to know the people more, and I found the children receptive and ready to learn. Some of them had no books at home, and they'd grown up without intellectual stimulation. I wanted them to succeed and I thought the key to their success was reading.

Although I enjoyed teaching at St. Michael's, in my second year at the convent, my life began to feel bleak and monotonous. Rising every day at 5:30—morning prayers—breakfast—going off in the van to St. Michael's—cleaning functions—chapel again—refectory again—the lack of connection among us.

Old doubts resurfaced and needled me until one day I was so overcome with blackness and despair that I felt as if I'd been knocked down by a tidal wave.

Seizing a moment when I could talk to my superior in the privacy of her office, I told her I wanted to leave.

"Did this *wanting to leave* come upon you suddenly?" she asked.

"Yes, Mother."

"Sister, you would be making a big mistake to leave," she told me. "Let me arrange for you to speak to a priest, and in the meantime, pray, Sister."

It was the same advice that I'd received from Mother Consolata in the novitiate—*Don't leave.* Mother arranged for me to consult with a Marist priest. I took the train from Providence to Westerly, where Father Parent met me at the tiny station and drove me to the Marist Monastery. There, in between puffs of smoke as he chain-smoked some unbeknown-to-me brand of cigarette, he said, "Sister, don't be so ready to take the escape hatch. Don't you think married people occasionally feel like throwing in the towel?"

I listened but was not convinced that a married person's conflict was equivalent to my own. I thanked him, and on the train ride back, I pondered my situation. I had no peace. I was ambivalent. I remembered Mother Consolata's words to me in the novitiate: "Do you want to turn your back on God?"

Maybe it was normal to feel a sense of ennui after a

number of years. Probably married couples, after a time, longed for freedom. I supposed this was the idea that Father Parent was trying to convey. But the analogy was imperfect.

My second vow precluded me from having an intimate relationship with another human being—even touching or embracing would take back the pledge of chastity that I had made.

Maybe it was this convent's institutional setting that set the tone for a lack of warmth. The new building, in spite of its comforts, was like a shell. Within the shell we were all engaged with our work, but we were not connected in a human way.

How would I face a lifetime of faithfulness to my vows? I wanted to be faithful but didn't know if I had the courage to continue. And so I prayed.

My feelings of confusion continued for days until gradually the dark cloud lifted. Again I had convinced myself by kneeling in front of the tabernacle that I had a true calling to the life.

In my second year there I heard that Sister Rosalie was coming to live at Prospect Street. I was thrilled. In all the years since I'd entered, we'd never lived together. And even though we'd be teaching in different schools—she at Holy Name and I at St. Michael's—we'd be part of the same community of sisters.

But Sister Rosalie was not happy about her transfer to Prospect Street. Not happy to leave her post in a small mining town in Pennsylvania where she'd been principal for two years. She had thrived on leadership and now she'd been sent back to the ranks to teach at Holy Name School, where the principal was a junior sister. The Sister Rosalie I had known before was outgoing and sociable. Now she stayed in her room much of the time.

"There's no respect for seniors," she said to me one day. "Why don't they line us all up and shoot us?"

I'd loved Sister Rosalie since my days at the convent boarding school when I was twelve. Back then her energy, her sense of humor, the way she clicked her tongue on the roof of her mouth to make a popping sound—everything about her charmed me. I loved the way she'd caressed her folded street veil, grasping it in both hands and pressing her lips to the thin voile.

Now after all these years, Sister Rosalie and I were, more than ever, connected—living in community—except that we were not connected. I didn't understand why she seemed so resentful of the young sisters. It was probably because, as a person with many gifts, she had not been given the recognition that was now being accorded to some of the younger ones. I tried to be supportive, but it became harder for me to spend time with her.

Soon after the school year began, I realized my father

was not well. Over the summer he had lost a significant amount of weight, and when my parents came to visit one day, his legs buckled under him. "I'm fine," he assured me. "Just a temporary thing." It was characteristic of him to deny that there was anything wrong.

Soon after their visit my mother phoned me. "Your father's not eating," she said. "Would you talk to him and ask him to go to the doctor?"

I'd been granted permission to go home for a day—an implementation of the new rules. In the more relaxed setting at home, I observed that my father was more frail than when I'd last seen him. "Dad," I said, "would you please see the doctor?"

The following Saturday my mother met me at La Salle after classes. My father had been to the doctor, and the news was not good. He had been diagnosed with esophageal cancer, and the doctor projected that he would barely last three months. It was a shock! Esophageal cancer. Inoperable. A death sentence. I should have suspected, from my father's outward appearance, that the diagnosis would be grave. But I was in denial, myself. I didn't want to believe my father was going to die.

I went numb. My mother was in grief, in need of comfort. We had just a few minutes together—the van was waiting to take me back to the convent. I put my arms around my mother and kissed her. "I'm so sorry, Mom, that I have to go. I'll get permission to come home."

When I got back to the convent, I went to my room, threw myself on the bed, and sobbed. Moans and shrieks came from my depths—almost frightening sounds that I didn't know were inside me. I loved my father more than anyone in the world, and to think that he would soon be gone from life filled my heart with intense sorrow.

I know that the sadness I felt that day eclipsed any feelings of sadness I experienced on the day of my father's death. My grieving was not only for the loss, but also for the suffering I knew he would endure until death released him from pain.

I wanted to go home on Saturdays. Since I would already be in Providence for morning classes, I thought that permission would be readily granted and I approached my superior.

Mother Mary Anastasia was the new superior at Prospect Street. She'd been at Sacred Hearts all her life—first as a student and later as the art teacher. I'd known her since I was twelve, when she'd been in charge of the high school boarders. She had a good sense of humor and the boarders liked her, although some of the sisters in community were surprised about *Sister* Mary Anastasia's elevation to the role of superior. Time would tell.

I asked permission to go home on Saturdays after class. My mother would meet me at La Salle and drive me the short distance to my parents' home on Walton Street, and my brother would drive me back to the convent in the evenings.

I had to steel myself for these visits—seeing my father bedridden, his body wasting away, a tee shirt covering the radiated skin on his chest. Hiding his obvious pain he would ask, "How are you, sweetheart?"

These visits were heartbreaking. My father was in denial and my mother was abusing alcohol. It was hard to keep tears back, and at times I couldn't—especially when he said to me one day, "Marion, I'm not worried about myself. It's your mother I'm concerned about."

As winter progressed my father's condition deteriorated. I knew visiting on Saturdays was not enough and I asked Mother Mary Anastasia to extend the visiting permission to include Wednesdays.

"Sister, you already see your father on Saturdays. You can't have more time than that. Your place is here with the sisters."

I took a breath. "Mother," I said, "my father is *dying*. I believe that my *place* is with my parents—to comfort them." And I added, "I think, if we're following Jesus, that's what He would do."

"Leaving the diocese on Sunday requires the bishop's permission," she said.

"All right, Mother, I'll be glad to call him."

"No, Sister. I'll make the call."

Never before had I argued with my superior—"the voice of God speaking." What I heard from the mouth of my superior was not God's voice, but a pharisaic rendering of rules. That encounter with my superior liberated me and gave me focus on what I saw as the primal reason for my existence as a religious. Apart from personal reason for the exemption—to give solace to my dying father—I think it was a cataclysmic moment for me with far-reaching changes in how I viewed my vocation.

The radiation had so burned my father's chest that the resulting seepage caused the skin to stick to his undershirt. I applied compresses of tea-soaked gauze and cut away little pieces at a time. My father did his best to appear jovial. "I'll be in Madison Square Garden next week," he said one time.

I continued to go home twice a week. When my father was hospitalized, I'd go with my mother to see him there. In the evening my brother Bob would drive me back to the convent in his old beat-up Mustang with a section of floor missing on the passenger's side. It was probably a good distraction to joke about seeing the ground beneath me.

No matter how late I arrived back at the convent, Sister Rosalie always wanted me to stop by her room so she could ask about my father. Often, before leaving home my mother would give me a mayonnaise jar filled with Gallo Brothers muscatel, and Sister Rosalie and I would sip the wine as I debriefed.

Visiting in another sister's room, especially after night prayer, was expressly forbidden—not to mention drinking wine. But somehow I didn't think of this as an infraction. Sister Rosalie was empathic. She'd had her own share of sorrow—witnessing the suffering of her brother to Parkinson's disease. She listened as I recounted the day.

It was painful to see my father declining each time I visited. He lost so much weight, he looked almost skel-etal, and toward the end, he had to be readmitted to the hospital. My mother and I were there on his last day when he called out to his dead mother. He struggled for breath. A nurse's aide came in the room, drew the curtains, and asked us to step outside. In a few seconds she came out to the corridor to tell us that my father had passed away. To this day I think of that, and wish I had stayed to hold my father, to give him my love before he drew his last breath.

It was April 10, 1965.

Some time after my father's death, my mother came to the Prospect Convent to see me. Mother Mary William expressed her sympathy and assured my mother that she would leave me at Prospect Street for another year, though I'd spend the summer in Puerto Rico, training for the Spanish apostolate in New York. My mother was touched by Reverend Mother's kindness and I, as well. It was heart-ening to see the more humane side of religious life.

As the school year at St. Michael's was winding down,

I began my preparations for the summer program in Puerto Rico at the Universidad Católica in Ponce.

The program would be conducted under the auspices of the Archdiocese of New York and under the aegis of Monsignor Fox, head of the Spanish Apostolate. I knew Monsignor Fox from having volunteered the previous summer for his inner city enrichment program. We'd had a week's orientation to prepare us for our work with the children. In our workshop we'd interacted with Joseph Fitzpatrick, S.J., a sociologist, and Daniel Berrigan, S.J., who would later be remembered as an anti-Vietnam War activist who spilled blood on draft records at the Pentagon—one of the Catonsville Nine. There was also a diocesan priest, Father Thompson, and a Trinitarian Sister, Sister Christina—a social worker. Sisters, brothers, and priests from multiple orders participated in the program.

Monsignor Fox was movie star handsome, and I think most of the nuns were half in love with him. But it wasn't only his looks that attracted everyone to him. He exuded unction, a spirit that communicated love—godly love. He genuinely loved people and he was dedicated to making people's lives better. Poor people had no better advocate. He delivered homilies in fluent Spanish.

I remember the first day that Monsignor Fox spoke to us as we were all gathered in a group. He said, "Don't think of working in 'Summer in the City' as something you are bringing to the people. You will get much more from them than the other way around."

I'd worked in East Harlem for the seven or eight weeks in the summer program, and we'd taken the children on field trips to Central Park and Randall's Island. We'd had block parties—closing off a street and setting makeshift tables with all kinds of contributed dishes from the neighborhood—*plátanos*, *quenepas*, *arroz*, even a pig roasting on a spit—right there on 107th Street.

We sang *Michael, row the boat ashore, alleluia… This land is my land… Where have all the flowers gone? Five hundred miles…* Under the direction of volunteer artists, some of the children painted murals on the otherwise dilapidated brick buildings in the neighborhood.

That summer in the city was my introduction to the culture of the Spanish population in East Harlem, and now I was excited about going to Puerto Rico to study the language and to learn more about the culture of the island.

The plane ride to Puerto Rico was thrilling. I'd never flown before, and that might have been a good thing because I had no idea that takeoff and landing are the two most critical parts of the flight. After being up in the air for approximately three hours, we touched down at the San Juan Airport.

From San Juan we were taken by bus to our quarters at the Catholic University in Ponce. Sister Maria Gregory (the only other sister from Holy Union) and I shared a dorm room.

We were in the company of probably a hundred religious—mainly sisters, but also some religious orders of Christian and Marist Brothers. Monsignor Fox gave the opening welcome and then we divided into groups for workshops. Father Dan (Berrigan) gave a workshop on poetry—he being a poet, himself.

In the mornings we attended language class. The teaching method was the same one used to teach the Foreign Service personnel and required a lot of rote memorization.

In the afternoons and evenings we had activities planned for us by Sister Christina. We went on trips all over the island—to El Yunque rain forest, to Barranquitas, Fajardo, Viejo San Juan, and La Perla—where people lived in the water in huts up on stilts. We went to Mayaguez—beautiful Mayaguez, with its flamboyan trees. Everywhere we went we found the people *simpático*, a key word used often by Monsignor Fox, who, more than anyone, was devoted to the people and to the culture. Another word we heard often was *dignidad*—dignity. No matter how humble or how poor, we were to remember a person's dignity.

One field trip I'll never forget was a bus trip into the mountains. The bus driver—a meat cutter—had been pressed into service that day when no other chauffeur could be found. The mountains in Puerto Rico are like corkscrews, with many twists and turns and no guardrails (at least there weren't any in 1965). Going up we braced ourselves as our bus, loaded with about forty of us, careened along the top of a precipice and maneuvered its way forward above the valley below—one slip away from hurtling us into the hereafter.

As we descended on the return trip, dusk gave way to semi-darkness and the driver put on the headlights. Gradually as the sun went down, we could no longer see out of the windows, and maybe it was just as well. The driver, we thought, was being extra careful. He seemed to be going slower—and then we, or someone in the front of the bus, realized that the headlights had gone out.

Now it was quiet on the bus. As the driver inched along, some of us took out our rosary beads and prayed Hail Marys. I saw Father Thompson open his leather-bound breviary. What psalm is he reading now, I wondered—*Out of the depths I have cried to Thee, O Lord, hear my prayer…*I prepared for my death. Having witnessed the treacherous passes by day, what would our chances be of surviving a plummet over a cliff—in a bus—with no headlights— driven by a meat cutter, I pondered.

It was a long, suspenseful ride that finally ended on *terra firma*. "It's a miracle," we all said.

Once we visited a leper colony on another island. I had previously read of Father Damien and his life with the lepers on Molokai (after many years of caring for the people, he contracted the disease and died there). But no photos or descriptions could prepare anyone for seeing real people with parts of their bodies ravaged by the disease. There was a man who had only a part of his nose, others whose bodies were badly disfigured. Sister Christina told us to shake hands with the people. There was only a risk, she said, of contracting the disease if you touched an open wound.

What amazed me was that the people there seemed happy—cheerful—as if they had everything to live for. I found it hard to think of them living in that habitat for the rest of their lives while for the rest of us it was only a visit.

Sister Christina arranged a steel band concert for our entertainment. The musicians were men doing time in a local prison. On salvaged oil drums and other improvised instruments, they made wonderful upbeat music.

After six or seven weeks in the program, we were sent in pairs to various parts of the island for *fieldwork*. The idea was to mingle with the people and practice the Spanish we'd learned. My partner was Sister Odile, an Immaculate Heart Sister. We were sent to Caguas to do census taking. Odile, from Ireland, had a keen sense of humor, and we made a great team. It was amusing to hear her speak Spanish with a bit of a brogue. In one of the houses we visited, a man asked us: *"Quieren ustedes comer unos niños?"* *Niños* we knew as the name for little boys. We falsely interpreted his question as: *Do you want to eat some little boys?* We didn't know that *niños* is also the word for miniature bananas.

After nine weeks the program ended and we went back to our respective communities—all the richer for our experience with Monsignor Fox, the staff, and the Puerto Rican people.

Returning to Prospect Street, full of the richness of the summer program in Puerto Rico, I knew, nevertheless, that I'd be teaching at St. Michael's for another year. It was a good thing for my mother that I would not be far away from her in Providence.

Though I had developed a fondness for the Spanish community in East Harlem that included Puerto Ricans, Central Americans, and South Americans (at that time), I, nevertheless, loved St. Michael's and my work with the children. And I was poised to begin another year teaching fifth grade there. I could wait for New York.

Back at the Prospect Street Convent, Sister Rosalie began to separate herself from the community—skipping recreation at times. She still complained about what she perceived as the young sisters' lack of respect for the seniors. It seemed that whenever I was with her, the conversation always turned to that theme. I wanted to help her but I didn't know how.

I prayed that I would find the right words to convey my concern without wounding her pride. Then one day I approached her. "Sister," I said, "you know, I wish I could help you. But I don't think I know how. What if you sought some professional counseling…?"

The words were scarcely out of my mouth when she erupted:

"Get out! Who do you think you are to talk to me like that? Get out!" She was screaming. I had bungled things. I hadn't meant to hurt her. For the next several days when I tried to approach her, she turned away. If our paths crossed in the corridor, she took another stairway to avoid me. There would be no rapprochement between us for many years.

I have thought since then that Sister Rosalie was depressed. She was very capable and had served two years as principal in the little mining town in Pennsylvania—only to come back to teach in an elementary school under another administrator. Also there was no outlet for her deep affection. I know I didn't give her any—so imbued was I with rules about attachment. That was how I saw my vow. I only wish I could have displayed more empathy. She must have wondered at what happened to her protégée.

1966–1967 New York

August 22, the feast of the Immaculate Heart of Mary, the day awaited by some with angst and others with hope— the day of the billets-doux. Following noon recreation all of us, fresh from summer school and retreat, assembled in the courtyard of the Prospect Street Convent, all eyes on Reverend Mother Mary William as she called out a litany of names. Sisters shuffled about in the lineup, receiving the small white envelopes (some in tears and others smiling). I already had an inkling and I waited in suspense. Suddenly I heard, "Sister Marion Joseph." I didn't lose a minute taking the card out of the envelope. Yes, yes, it said what I wanted. "St. Francis de Sales." I was going to New York!

I'd lived at the New York convent when I volunteered for Monsignor Fox's program in Spanish Harlem. I was thrilled to return now as a teacher at St. Francis de Sales, where I'd gotten to know many of the children and their parents. The parish, once a bastion of first generation and

Irish immigrants, had turned over to a largely Spanish-speaking community of Puerto Ricans and émigrés from South America.

I would live just outside the boundary of East Harlem in the former residence of the Cartier jewelers. Situated on East 96th Street between Fifth and Madison, close to Central Park, it was a Parisian-styled townhouse reminiscent of *hôtels particuliers* in France. The dichotomy of living in a five-story townhouse while the majority of our students lived in the projects was not lost on me, but the building did not belong to the sisters and had been purchased by the parish for use as a convent.

Stripped of most of its elegant trappings, the house itself was architecturally beautiful. Heroic-size wooden doors enclosed the inner courtyard from public view, and a small grilled window in one of the doors opened to survey visitors. When cars arrived both doors opened to reveal the long, narrow driveway—its yellow face bricks fastidiously laid out in a herringbone pattern.

At the far end, inside the garage was a device not unlike a lazy Susan, designed to spin the Cartier's vehicle around in forward direction. I had never seen it work. Maybe the electric switch had been disconnected or was in disrepair, for we always had to have someone as a lookout as drivers backed their way out into the street.

Inside the courtyard the entrance to the house was through a heavy glass door, framed in decorative wrought iron. Stepping inside a narrow vestibule, a visitor would face another filigreed glass door that opened into a large foyer. The polished floor was a striking diamond pattern of black-and-white marble. But the focal point of the room was a veined marble staircase with an iron balustrade that spiraled up to the third level. According to French custom the ground floor is the *rez-de-chaussée,* and the next level is the *prémière étage* or *first.* But as Americans we counted the ground floor as first.

A lamp table was the sole furnishing in the foyer except for a built-in telephone booth enclosed by a cream-colored door with gold leaf accents. Beyond the foyer was a small anteroom whose back wall featured a large mirror framed in gold leaf. And juxtapositioned to the mirror was an elevator—its brass accordion gate hidden behind a painted wooden door that matched the décor of the foyer.

Large paneled doors with brass knobs opened onto the parlor. The walls of palest yellow, accented by crown molding, were offset by the coffered ceiling in gold leaf. Against one wall a marble fireplace with curved mantel was reflected in the long gilt-edged mirror opposite. Sheer curtains covered the floor-to-ceiling casement windows, and gold draperies shut out the din of 96th Street.

The kitchen, in the rear of the house, boasted a mosaic floor of white diamond-shaped tile. A bay window overlooked the courtyard, and in the center of the room, a rectangular table stood like an island for meal preparation.

Tall built-in cabinets along the back wall displayed the chinaware. A pantry was stocked with nonperishable foods such as cereals, cookies, crackers, flour, sugar, and canned goods. A restaurant-sized refrigerator stored dairy products and other short-lived foods, while the freezer compartment kept meats and other commodities.

To the rear of the kitchen, in a hallway, was a dumbwaiter whose frayed ropes sometimes broke on ascent, causing it to seesaw. Dishes spun around and crashed into each other, spewing mashed potatoes and peas all over the shelves and creating what looked like a dog's dinner. Somehow we managed to repair the damage, and no matter how frustrating the occasional mishaps, we continued to use the dumbwaiter because it was better than hauling food-laden trays to the second-floor refectory.

The refectory, where we had meals, was one of two rooms on the second floor. At the top of the marble staircase, turning right, you entered the dining room. Along the back wall were two marble and bronze fountains each with the carved head of the god Bacchus. In the Cartier's time, on special occasions like birthdays, I imagine Dom Pérignon must have flowed liberally through the open mouths of the gods. The hook-up had long since been disconnected, and we did not drink champagne.

French doors, fenced in by an iron railing, faced the courtyard below. Too small for use as a balcony, a narrow ledge ran the width of the doors, and only pigeons alighted there. They made a mess with their droppings, and once Sister Kathleen Joseph was reported to the Audubon Society by a woman in one of the apartments abutting our courtyard. The woman had observed Sister Kathleen taking away pigeon eggs from the ledge. I never thought of pigeons as an endangered species. Anyway, nothing came of the incident, and to my recollection we didn't see any more eggs on the ledge.

Our chapel—once the Cartier's ballroom—was opposite the dining room and separated by a rotunda. In this opulent setting where once society people had danced on the parquet floor, there now stood thirteen prie-dieux and chairs. The walls were paneled in walnut, and chandeliers hung from the ceiling. Our linen-covered altar faced us, and a bronze tabernacle to the left of the altar housed the Sacred Host. Near the casement windows a red cylindrical sanctuary lamp burned all day and night. Passersby, not knowing the structure was a convent, might have taken it for the house of a madam.

At times we had to open the windows to change the air, but even with the windows closed, sounds of the city were all around us: sanitation trucks in early morning, fire engines sirens screaming as hose and ladder trucks zoomed past us to douse a fire. Ambulances on their way to Mt. Sinai… Periodically a raucous male voice from a neighboring apartment building blasted us with a litany of invectives:

"Black-skirted fairies…fucking whores…goddamned fucking whores."

In counterpoint we chanted the Litany of the Blessed Virgin:

> Mother most pure…pray for us.
> Mother most chaste… pray for us.
> Mother inviolate… pray for us.

Mother Mary Declan was the new superior at 96th Street. Some of us had known her as Sister Mary Declan when she was senior to us in the novitiate. As a postulant I'd observed her kindness and generosity, and I'd looked up to her as a role model. After some of the past difficulties I'd had with certain superiors, I felt blessed to have Mother Mary Declan at the helm.

We were thirteen sisters counting our superior, and we were a mixed community of ages—some of the sisters had been at St. Francis for a number of years, but half a dozen of us had known each other in the novitiate, and we were bonded by the experience. Altogether it was a cohesive community, and collectively we had an abundance of talent and energy. Everyone was committed to inspiring the students to reach their potential. It was an exciting time, a time of transition, for although the Church itself had been undergoing transformation since the convening of Vatican II in 1962, little in the way of reform had trickled down to our convents in four years. Change was in the air, Pope John XXIII, before his death, called for more openness and more humanity.

Still clothed in our 1860s habits, we discussed modifications that would be more in consonance with the twentieth century. We experimented with different models of dress and shorter veils. We were somewhat giddy as we doffed our old habits and donned our new clothes (like the solstice song—*don we now our gay apparel*).

Sister Richard Marie (Pat) and I shaved our legs for the first time in years so we could wear nylons. We tossed our black oxfords after we shopped the boutiques on 34th Street for modern shoes. Pat found a pair of discounted I. Magnin flats with bows across the instep. I bought high-heeled pumps that I later returned to the store, realizing that high heels and veils were incongruous. We had to learn. After so many years of covering our bodies in armor, we were just beginning to express our femininity.

The superiors general of all the congregations were enjoined to follow the new mandates of the ecclesiastical Congregation of the Religious. Gradually our ancient constitutions were being revised to meet contemporary needs.

Belgian Cardinal Joseph Suenens advocated in his 1962 book, *The Nun in the Modern World*, that the active orders—teaching, nursing, etc.—adapt their external appearance, but also their rules of governance.

One small change that we welcomed was the allowance for leisure time. In the novitiate we'd been taught that our time belonged to the Congregation and that we had no right to spend any time in our own pursuits. For years, in addition to teaching Sunday school, we were obliged to count the weekly church collection for the priests. The rest of the day we wrote lesson plans and prepared our classes while waiting turns for a conference with the superior.

Some enlightened theologians such as Hans Küng realized that the spiritual and mental health of the sisters would be greatly enhanced if they were allowed some autonomy. A directive came from our Mother General declaring Sunday a free day. Mother Mary Declan gave us subway tokens. We could go out in the city. We must have had a small amount of cash—in keeping with our vow of poverty—and, no doubt, on return from our excursions, we handed in what we did not use.

We took advantage of free or low-cost art performances at the Cooper Union. Occasionally we took in a film downtown. Pat and I saw a screening of *Who's Afraid of Virginia Woolf* with Richard Burton and Liz Taylor—a stark contrast to *The Sound of Music* that we'd seen in Fall River. On another occasion Pat and I went to see the stage production of *Fiddler on the Roof*. After the performance, as we were leaving the theatre, two older women looked at

Pat and me (even in our modified habits, there was no mis-taking us as Catholic nuns) and one of them, seemingly surprised that we'd go to a Jewish-themed musical, said, "Oh, they let you out to see this?" The women were charm-ing and we assured them that, yes, nuns could go to Jewish plays, and besides, we loved it.

Silence during meals was abrogated, and we enjoyed conviviality at suppertime when we were all in the refec-tory. We moved the four separate tables together so we could face each other and converse more easily on such topics as we'd read in the *National Catholic Reporter*.

Almost every night a group of us, dressed in our bath-robes, went down to the kitchen to share and explore ideas about new directions for the Congregation—in light of what we were learning from the lectures at Fordham and from reading journals about the changes in the Church. We'd been schooled in Mother Consolata's strict interpre-tation of the Holy Rule. But now, in the spirit of the Second Vatican Council, we were trying to reconcile our novice mistress' teachings with the needs of our new apostolate. Our minds had been opened, and we were processing information from learned theologians such as Ivan Illich, Hans Küng, and Cardinal Suenens.

Our convent was a microcosm of the world outside. Some sisters, Mother Declan included, were clinging to traditional customs, while others among us clamored for change. The kitchen group belonged to the latter persuasion, and although we did not knowingly exclude anyone from our nightly gatherings, those who espoused more conservative values chose not to attend our soirées.

Such an assembly would have been unthinkable under the old regime, particularly in Fall River. Yet it seemed so natural to us that we didn't seek our superior's permission. We enjoyed camaraderie with each other, and we dispensed with our religious names, addressing each other by our given names—Hildy, Mary Ellen, Jane, Pat, Helen, and Marion.

On Saturdays we took the subway to the Bronx and attended the Jesuit Mass at Fordham. All present were invited to enter the sanctuary (the section traditionally reserved for the priests and altar boys) and participate in the liturgy. Some students played guitar, and we sang a variety of hymns, but sometimes a Beatles song like *"All you need is love…"* We'd indeed been invited into the mystery of the Mass, and we felt more connected there than we did in the gothic structure at St. Francis.

We received the Communion host and also drank from the chalice—something not countenanced by the Archdiocese of New York. We left there feeling spiritually refreshed. It was a positive experience that we shared with all present—nuns and laity.

One night during the evening meal, Mother Mary Declan informed us that earlier in the day she'd attended a meeting convened by Cardinal Spellman for the religious superiors of the archdiocese. The cardinal was displeased, she said, about nuns attending the Fordham Masses, and he wished the superiors to express this to their sisters.

"But, Mother," I gasped, "that Mass is the highlight of my week. I wouldn't want to give it up."

Mother looked pained, but said nothing. Then Pat spoke up: "Mother, can you leave the Church and stay in the convent?"

Mother Mary Declan's face contracted. I think she didn't know whether Pat was just trying to add some levity to the situation or whether she was serious. The chasm was widening between us—between Mother Mary Declan, the newly minted superior who wanted to adhere to old ideas, and those of us who were now rejecting some of the old ways. I suppose she might have thought us rebellious and maybe we were. We had gotten a taste for the new theology, and we were hungry for more.

After Pat's remark there was silence. We put our forks down and stopped eating. I felt sorry for Mother Mary Declan. She was a kind person, but she was fearful of change.

St. Francis de Sales School was located on East 97th Street between Lexington and Third. Mother Mary Declan, herself, had attended St. Francis Grammar School when the parish was largely made up of immigrants from Ireland. Her mother had come from Donegal.

To accommodate the burgeoning number of students, certain grades were duplicated. Sister Kathleen Joseph (Jane) and I taught fifth grade in adjoining classrooms. We were bonded since the novitiate, and we'd lived in together at St. William's. Now in our teaching we collaborated as a team.

At Christmastime we took our two classes—just shy of eighty students—to see the decorations at Gimbels and Macy's. We filled two subway cars! Some of those kids had never been downtown, and many had never been too far afield of the projects where they lived. To see their faces light up as they gazed at the snowcapped villages and moving figurines in the display windows of Macy's made our pleasure greater than theirs.

After Christmas vacation the weather turned frigid. Sister Kathleen Joseph and I worked out a plan to take our kids ice-skating on the lagoon at East 110th Street. We got parental permission slips, and on Friday afternoons at dismissal time, we lined up the skating patrol and off we went to the entrance at Flower and Fifth. Most of the kids did not own skates, but for a modest fee they could rent them as we did.

Snaking our way along the curvature of the lagoon, we stopped at the rental shack, put on our skates, and ventured out onto the ice. Sister Kathleen and I, our veils flapping in the wind, must have looked like two flying nuns à la Sally Field.

The cold weather continued, and the ice-skating patrol became a ritual. Gradually as word got out, more kids from other classes followed. Sometimes as I glanced back over my shoulder, I'd see a stream of kids trailing along behind us, and I'd feel like Moses leading the people into the Promised Land.

In June we sent notes home to the parents requesting permission to take the kids to Brighton Beach. Again we filled two subway cars. The kids wore their bathing suits under shorts and tops. They behaved admirably, though it was a long ride and I think we had to change trains for Brooklyn.

On arrival at the beach, we sat them all down and laid out the rules. They had to stay with their "buddy" as previously arranged. They could go in the water but not beyond a certain point. If they wanted to buy hot dogs or drinks at the stand, they had to report to us before and after so we knew where they were.

Those kids reveled in the experience. At the end of the day, we did roll call. One girl, Barbara, had gone missing. We were frantic with worry. Then, ambling along the beach, we spied Barbara, tears streaming down her face. We ran and scooped her up. Whether we scolded her or whether we were so relieved to find her unharmed, I don't remember. Now when I think of the risks we took…all I can say is the angels must have been with us that day.

Sometime in the middle of that year, Reverend Mother Mary William's term expired and a new provincial was elected. I'd been fond of Mother Mary William. She had a breadth of spirit. She was kind and compassionate. As I tried to picture Reverend Mother Thomasina in the role of provincial, I remembered the time I'd been a student in her Victorian Lit class. There was no subject I liked more than literature, and I had reveled in Thomas Hardy's *Tess of the D'Urbervilles*. Writing that final exam at the end of the summer session was fun for me because I'd loved reading the book.

I was one of the first to finish writing the answers to the exam questions. I put down my pen and strode to the front of the room. Sister Thomasina did not look up as I deposited my blue book in the tray on her desk.

It was only after everyone had floated out of the music building (where we had classes) that I heard parts of a discussion about the exam. Realizing then that I had missed something, I ran back inside the building. "Sister," I said, "I must not have noticed that there was another page of questions…could I please take a makeup exam? I know the material…"

"No, Sister! Part of taking an exam is following through. If you didn't turn the page over, you have to take the consequences."

"But, Sister…this will affect my final grade. Please."

"No, Sister."

Now Sister Thomasina was replacing Reverend Mother Mary William, and she would be my provincial for the next six years. I couldn't help comparing her to Mother Mary William, who was compassionate and had a breadth of spirit.

According to the Holy Rule, provincial superiors were required to visit each house once a year to assess the spiritual and financial status of the community and to interview each sister as well as the local superior.

Around the middle of March, Reverend Mother Thomasina came to 96th Street to conduct her visitation. The interviews took place in a small room on a floor we called "two and a half" (because the elevator didn't stop there).

I walked in and closed the door behind me. The interviews were private.

"Hello, Reverend Mother," I said.

She was seated in a chair, a small notebook on her lap. "Sister." She gestured for me to take the chair facing her. She opened the conversation by asking me the usual questions—how was I getting along in the community…my physical and spiritual health…my work with the children. I assured her I had no health problems and I believed my spiritual life was healthy as well. I loved teaching the children and I was happy in the community.

"Is there anything you want to tell me?" she asked.

"No, Reverend Mother," I said, "but I am excited about the prospect of some reforms in religious life."

"All change is slow, Sister. You must be patient."

"Yes, Reverend Mother," I said.

Then I glanced at my watch and saw that it was 4:40. "Oh, Reverend Mother," I said, "would you excuse me? I need to go to the Sanchez home by five o'clock. They've invited me to dinner."

Reverend Mother's face registered surprise. "You know we don't do that," she said.

"Yes, Reverend Mother, I know. But Rosita is in my class, and when her mother invited me, I accepted the invitation."

"Then, Sister, I will not forbid you to go. But it is my wish that you do not."

"Reverend Mother, thank you for not forbidding me. And, please, I hope you understand. I feel I must go."

Then, slowly, I rose from my chair, taking in at a glance her impassive expression. "Thank you, Reverend Mother," I said in parting. And I opened the door, leaving it ajar for the next sister.

Fordham, Summer, 1967

In summer of 1967 I enrolled in a program at Fordham for a master's degree in religious education. Living on campus opened a larger milieu from that of 96th Street. The interchanges and discussions with other participants exposed me to a pool of ideas and new concepts of theology. Interesting to note is that many of the required course readings were from textbooks written by Protestant theologians (score one for the Jesuits for their openness). We read *Radical Theology and the Death of God* by Thomas Altizer, *Honest to God* by the Anglican Bishop John Robinson, *The Secular City* by Harvey Cox, and *Letters and Papers from Prison* by Dietrich Bonhoeffer.

The readings were very intellectual, and I read certain passages several times in order to comprehend their meaning. Reflecting on what I gleaned from the writings of these credentialed theologians caused me to reexamine theology that I'd embraced since childhood.

The summer session was a watershed for me. For one thing I began to reject the idea of a personal God. Since the age of six when I'd been taught by nuns in parochial school, I'd believed in the *triple-decker universe*—a concept debunked by the *God Is Dead* theologians. That idea, they said, belonged to a time when man's understanding of cosmology was primitive. The idea that God was not a projection *out there* began to make sense to me. As I pondered these ideas, I strove to reconcile the new concepts with what I'd believed since childhood.

As I got deeper into the readings, I had more questions than answers. I found that I no longer believed in the transubstantiation (the doctrine Catholics believe that holds

Jesus is substantially—not metaphorically—present in the Consecrated Host). I stopped believing in the virgin birth of Jesus, the Resurrection, and the ascent into heaven.

Technically, I suppose I was no longer a Catholic in good standing. In the words of the Apostles Creed (which I'd recited from memory at Mass since the age of reason), the doctrines concerning the *virgin birth, the resurrection, the ascent into heaven*— these doctrines were irrefutable. My foundation was crumbling.

I'd always believed in a transcendent God, a God who listened to me. I had consecrated my life to the Person of Jesus Christ. I was searching for answers. What was happening to my faith?

1967–1968 New York

After the summer session at Fordham, I joined the other sisters in New England for vacation and retreat. Still struggling to resolve my lack of faith, I decided to give myself another year to sort things out. In September, back at 96th Street, I continued to confront my misgivings in the doctrines of the Catholic Church. I recalled Mother Consolata saying that the greatest battles were fought on the battleground of the soul. Now as I wrestled with my demons, I comprehended the meaning. A priest I consulted told me he had no words of wisdom. He listened sympathetically but said, "Sister, this is a personal crisis of faith and one that you have to work out for yourself."

And so I lived in community, a daily communicant at Mass, chanting the Holy Office and joining in communal prayer while inwardly struggling to make sense of a life dedicated to the teaching of doctrine I no longer believed.

I stepped into the chapel and sat down at my prie-dieu

without genuflecting in front of the altar. Mother Mary Declan shot me a look. Since I no longer believed in the Blessed Sacrament, I thought it hypocritical to genuflect. Mother never mentioned it, though I think she was somewhat startled by my non-observance of the rubrics. And, at times, my vocal expressions of throwing off some of the rules upset her. Declan was good. I'd liked her since our shared novitiate days. But I felt she was too constrained.

I'd been raised in a family of practicing Catholics. My great-uncle, Father John Sullivan, had been pastor of St. Matthew's in Cranston, Rhode Island. Throughout my parochial school education, I'd never questioned the Church's teachings, and here I was after sixteen years in the convent confronting beliefs that I'd held since childhood.

Yet I was happy in the camaraderie of the sisters who shared the same belief in aggiornamento. Cardinal Suenens's book *The Nun in the Modern World* and the ideas generated from visiting theologians at Fordham had influenced the way I saw my role in an active apostolate.

We watched the nightly news on television and saw the brutality of war—graphic photos of the dead and wounded night after night appeared on the screen. Unlike today's reporting, the news and images of the wounded were not sanitized. We marched for Civil Rights and against the US involvement in the Vietnam War.

On Christmas Eve Pat and I were in the kitchen

preparing a special dinner for the next day's feast. I can see myself standing at the rectangular table, my hands sticky from kneading breadcrumbs, sausage meat, and onions for the turkey stuffing. Pat was at the sink washing the pans when Mother Mary Declan made her entrance.

"Midnight Mass will be in the church tonight instead of the convent," she said.

"Oh, we're not going, Mother. Sister Richard Marie and I are going to Mass at Emmaus House." We didn't even think about asking permission. Mother turned and walked out of the kitchen.

Pat and I exchanged glances. Midnight Mass at Emmaus (a settlement house run by two Dutch priests) trumped the traditional.

We took the train and got off at the nearest stop to Emmaus House—I think it was somewhere around East 112th. The door to the brownstone opened to a long, steep staircase that led to a large room filled with people. The two priests, dressed in neatly pressed brown suits, were leaning against the fireplace—one smoking a pipe and the other smiling as he talked to some young people.

After a while the priests made a move to ready everything for the Mass. A tray with a freshly baked baguette was passed hand-to-hand. "If you're planning to receive communion," one of the priests said, "break off a piece of bread and place it on the tray."

The Mass proceeded—but not like any Mass you

would encounter in a church. A young woman with long hair and a flowered dress strummed her guitar and sang, "All ya need is love…dah da dah da da…all ya need is love, LOVE, love is all ya need."

At the peace offering, instead of the customary handshake, everyone threw their arms around the people standing near them and hugged as they gave each other the kiss of peace.

After the Mass Pat and I mingled with the thirty or so people gathered there as coffee and refreshments were passed around. Then we said good-bye, thanked the priests, and let ourselves out.

Christmas Day had begun. It was nearly two in the morning and the street was deserted. I don't remember if we caught a train at that hour or walked the sixteen blocks to 96th Street. When we let ourselves into the convent with our key, we heard merrymaking coming from the refectory.

All the sisters were gathered around a table, opening presents. They looked up as we entered the room, but Mother averted her eyes from us. Amidst all the decorations and poinsettias—the candy cane wrapping papers strewn about on the floor—a pall fell over the group. For Pat and me it was an anticlimax to Christmas Eve.

We went to bed and rose later on Christmas morning to attend the children's Mass in church. After breakfast Mother Mary Declan, to my surprise, handed me a large box covered with shiny paper and tied in a red bow. "This is for you, Marion," she said.

I undid the wrapping and opened the package. There inside was a pair of white figure skates with silver blades. "So you don't have to rent skates at the lagoon anymore." That was Declan. "Thank you, Mother," I said as I hugged her.

Pope John XXIII had died in 1963 and was succeeded by Paul VI. The reforms of Vatican II seemed slowed down under the new pope. Nevertheless our Mother General in Rome had asked our communities to submit suggestions for revising our Constitutions. There was disagreement on how certain norms should be implemented. Those on the more liberal side shocked those who were reluctant to part with the familiar.

One day Mother pulled me aside and said, "Marion, I wish you would shut your mouth. You're upsetting some of the sisters."

"I think some of them need to be upset, Mother," I said.

I hadn't meant to be defiant or rude, but I was frustrated with the unwillingness of some to generate ideas for revision of the Rule. I felt they needed to be jarred out of their complacency. And, I thought, if they had issues, they should have spoken to me instead of to Mother.

Occasionally Fordham hosted guest lecturers such as Cardinal Suenens of Belgium (*The Nun in the Modern*

World), Ivan Illich of Cuernavaca, and Hans Küng, the Swiss theologian. Those of us who attended regularly were hungry for insight offered by these learned theologians, and we were ready to share the positive messages with the other sisters and with our students.

While many nuns informed themselves on the aggiornamento of Vatican II, it seemed to me that some of the diocesan priests had not, and they were still stuck on fire and brimstone. The redheaded curate, Father O'Toole, at St. Francis came to my classroom one Monday morning, demanding my list of students who'd missed the Sunday Children's Mass.

"I don't have a list, Father," I said.

"And why not, Sister?"

"Because, Father, I won't embarrass my students in front of their peers."

"What? Well, Sister, this is Monsignor's order. You're flying in the face of Monsignor's orders."

"I don't think so, Father," I said. "I'm following my conscience."

And with that Father O'Toole of the flaming hair stormed out of the room in a huff. He probably reported me to the pastor but I didn't care.

As the school year drew to a close, one of the sisters suggested a picnic on Fire Island. Fire Island! Famous, I knew, as a place where homosexual men hung out—so I wondered why Jane picked it, but it seemed not to matter. Mother gave permission and a sign-up sheet was tacked to the bulletin board.

Out of thirteen sisters only six were on board to go—the others offering a variety of excuses. The six of us from the kitchen soirée group were going: Hildy, Mary Ellen, Pat, Helen, Jane, and me.

Pat, the only one among us with a New York driver's license, borrowed a station wagon from a parishioner. She'd maneuvered it into the narrow driveway, and there it stood waiting for us. We had our brown bag lunches and were ready to depart when I said, "Look, I have an idea. There are lots of cartons (waiting for distribution) of summer clothes in the garage. Why don't we take some and change here instead of on the beach?"

"Oh, no," said Mary Ellen. "Mother will be upset."

"Listen, it'll be a lot easier than changing at Fire Island. We'll take our habits with us and change back before we come home."

It was decided. We dressed from an assorted collection of shorts and culottes. With our cropped hair and mismatched outfits, we probably looked as if we'd just escaped from the loony bin. But we were off to Fire Island in the Ford station wagon.

As Pat turned on Madison Avenue, we looked out the windows, seeing our neighborhood from a different vantage point. We went over the Triborough Bridge, but I didn't keep track after that. I suppose we had to cross the Causeway to get to the island. Everyone was talking and recounting stories that made us laugh. Then we were there.

We picked a site and were surprised that no one was around. Maybe we had frightened any would-be guests away. It was a beautiful sunny day and we were lucky to be fanned with ocean breezes. We enjoyed the day off and shared our picnic lunch.

Before we left 96th Street for the island, Mother Mary Declan had given permission for us to go later to Jane's (Sister Kathleen Joseph's) house on Long Island. Jane was soon to leave the Congregation and needed to store some books and papers at her family's home.

Still wearing our funny clothes—because in our haste we'd forgotten to take our habits with us—we arrived at Jane's family home in Patchogue in late afternoon. Jane's mother welcomed us and plied us with liberal amounts of alcohol in the form of cocktails. The sweet drinks tasted like soda pop and we kept drinking. When we said we needed to go, Mrs. Costello asked us to stay until Jane's father came home from work. A few more cocktails derailed our rational thinking, and we agreed to wait.

"Please stay," said Mrs. Costello. "You know my husband just can't accept that Jane is leaving. If you could explain it to him…"

Jane, in the meantime, had gone out to the garage to get packing boxes. From a bending position, as she stood up, a large rusty nail protruding from the wall caught her on the forehead, opening a deep gash. The wound bled so profusely, her mother had to take her for emergency care. This sobered us up sufficiently so that we realized the lateness of the hour and were aghast that we'd forgotten to call Mother Mary Declan. Mr. Costello still had not come home.

We dialed the convent and Mother answered the phone. She was furious that we hadn't called earlier. "I've been so worried," she said. Then we told her about Jane.

"Let me know when she gets back from the hospital," she said. "And don't drive back to the city tonight. Wait and come back tomorrow morning, and one of you stay with Sister until she's able to travel."

Jane had had to get stitches, but the doctor said she would heal. We talked with Mr. Costello and tried to reassure him that Jane was making the right decision.

That night we slept three to a bed and laughed like fools all night. Mary Ellen, Hildy, and I were sandwiched into a double-sized rope bed, and we kept rolling into one another and giggling. "Go to sleep," said Mary Ellen. "We'll never be able to get up in the morning."

The alarm at 5:30 woke us. We hustled to dress—once more in our motley borrowed clothes—before swallowing some coffee and muffins that Jane's mother provided.

In the car, the four of us—Pat, Mary Ellen, Hildy, and

I—waved good-bye to Mrs. Costello, who stood on the back porch blowing kisses.

As we turned onto South Ocean Avenue on our way back to the city, the mood was more somber. Mary Ellen was concerned about Mother's reaction to our wearing secular clothes.

"Don't worry, Mary Ellen," I said. "Mother will be relieved to know that Jane is okay, and she'll be happy that nothing else bad happened."

"I don't know," Mary Ellen said.

"We'll go in the back door," Pat said, "and change our clothes right away."

We hardly talked after that. Pat moved the wagon onto Grand Central Parkway, and eventually we were on FDR Drive. Arriving at 96th Street, we opened the wooden doors and drove into the courtyard. Gathering our belongings we opened the door to the kitchen. There at the small rectangular table, sitting alone and eating cereal—our superior! We hadn't expected that. "We're back, Mother."

Mother Mary Declan did not look up. The four of us took the elevator to the fifth floor.

"That was not right," said Mary Ellen. "I'm going to confront Mother."

"Don't do it," Pat said. "Let it go."

After supper Mary Ellen, Pat, Hildy and I were on

wash-up. We bantered and laughed as we reviewed the events of the past twenty-four hours. In the midst of mirth Mother Mary Declan entered the kitchen from the side door.

Looking at no one in particular she announced she'd reported our infraction to the provincial, and that on Sunday the four of us would appear before Reverend Mother. We would go by train to Providence and take a bus from there to Fall River. Then she turned abruptly into the hallway. We heard the click of the elevator gate and the hum of the motor.

For a few seconds we stood suspended as we registered this denunciation. We'd been summoned to the motherhouse to defend ourselves for something we'd done with no malice. The shock of it caused us to stand immobile, much like the freeze frame of a film. Then we burst out laughing. "They're going to spend money for four train tickets."

On Sunday morning we boarded the train to Providence. Turning the coach seats facing each other, we settled in for the journey. I remember our outbursts of laughter, and I wondered if we were making a spectacle of ourselves in front of the other passengers.

Mother Mary Declan had remained cool since our return from Patchogue, and barely spoken to us. Now we were on our way to the Inquisition. But as we played back the kitchen scene and thought of our superior reporting us to the provincial, the consensus was that Declan had overreacted.

From Union Station in Providence we boarded the Bonanza bus to downtown Fall River and walked up the hill to 492 Rock Street. At the front door we paused to regain composure and rang the bell. The heavy wooden door sprang open and before us stood Mother Mary Declan. (We learned later that she'd taken the shuttle from La Guardia).

We were ushered into the parlor and directed to sit on a long divan facing Reverend Mother Thomasina, who stood stone-faced, flanked on either side by her two councilors—Sister Therese Anna and Sister Celine Lucille.

It seemed a cross between theatre of the absurd and fifteenth century auto-da-fé. The interrogation began:

Did we not know that the Rule forbade the removal of the holy habit?

"Yes, Reverend Mother," I said, "but it's against the law to change clothes on Fire Island."

"Which rule takes precedence?"

I don't recall how we answered that one.

Sister Therese Anna lectured us on obedience to the Rule and we were duly chastened for our recalcitrant behavior. Mother Mary Declan aired some long held grievances against us. We listened to the charges and accepted the rebukes. Then the tribunal adjourned.

It was late when we got to Manhattan. Emerging from the underground on 96th Street we walked past St Francis de Sales, crossed Madison and headed north to number 15.

It had been a long day.

Without Ceremony

At the end of the academic year most of the sisters dispersed for summer study. Mother Mary Declan was off to Providence College and I returned to Fordham, still wrestling with doubts about Catholic doctrine. I immersed myself in course readings and classes. Three Holy Union sisters from New England were on campus and we enjoyed camaraderie

But by mid-July I realized that my status as a religious sister was incompatible with my disbelief. My companions were supportive about my decision to leave the Congregation. Sister John Alicia said, "Hey, let's have a party."

I remember sitting in one of the nicely furnished Jesuit parlors sipping Scotch as we celebrated my future. "Find a cosmetic boutique around 42nd Street," Sister John Alicia said. "Have them show you how to do make-up."

At the 96th Street Convent, I sat down at the little knee-hole table in the hallway on three outside the community room and stared at the black rotary phone—the New York number visible through the isinglass casing—Sacramento 2-5108. *Sacramento*—perhaps a more fitting telephone exchange for a group of religious women than Murray Hill 5 or Butterfield 8.

I drew a breath and leaned forward to pick up the receiver. I put my index finger into one of the little numbered holes and began dialing the provincial house in Fall River. In a heightened state of alert, I was conscious of the *whirring* sound each time the rotary dial snapped back into place.

After a pause I heard *rring...rring...rring*. The wait seemed interminable and now I was getting a queasy feeling in my stomach. The ringing was replaced by a high- pitched voice coming over the wire, cobbling words together: holyunionprovincialate. It was Mother Thomasina herself.

"Good afternoon, Reverend Mother," I said. "Sister Marion Joseph here."

I pictured her sitting at her desk in the large front room at 492 Rock, and though she was miles away, I felt my stomach tighten.

"Yes, Sister?"

I paused. "Reverend Mother," I began—and I'd rehearsed in my head what I was about to say—"Reverend Mother, I need to be dispensed from my vows. I...I..."

"Well, I don't think you can. The Pope isn't granting dispensations right now."

"Mm, Reverend Mother, I…I'd like to do it the right way. I've decided."

No sound from her end. After a few moments she said, "Well, you'll need to write a letter to the Holy Father explaining why you want the dispensation. The letter has to be written on official stationery with the seal of the Congregation. I'll send it to you along with the protocol. After you've written the letter, send it back to me."

"Thank you, Reverend Mother."

"God bless you, Sister."

God bless you, Sister?! I held the receiver in my hand until I heard the click. Though I'd made my decision and taken the first step in the process, I was hurt by Reverend Mother's perfunctory response. I'd been a member of the Congregation in good standing for sixteen years, and I thought she might have asked what precipitated my desire to leave.

I recalled other times I'd wanted to leave and my superiors implored me to seek spiritual counsel—Mother Consolata, Mother Gabriel Clare, and Mother Mary William. Well, this was Mother Thomasina. Maybe she thought I was a renegade. Some of my ideas, I know, had startled her. There was the time when she came on visitation and I'd said, "Reverend Mother, why not close some of the big churches and have Mass in storefronts like the evangelicals?" I'd said this not to shock her but because I truly believed that we had to find a way to strip some of the excess formality of the Church and reach out to people of other cultures. She had looked at me aghast when I said this. On another occasion I said, "I think we should stop teaching the Ten Commandments and focus more on the teachings of Jesus."

I suppose she thought I had gone too far and was over-stepping the elements of the Holy Rule. But maybe it was just Mother Thomasina being Mother Thomasina. It was okay. I was already composing the letter in my head.

The letter would be a mere formality. In my heart I didn't want to be a nun anymore. Sixteen years of doubts—recommitments—doubts again. Now it was fin-ished. Ironically the last two years at 96th Street had been my happiest convent years. I loved teaching at St. Francis and hoped that my teaching would make a difference in the lives of my students. I had received from the Puerto Rican people more than I had given. I knew I would miss the unction that came from their openness and generosity of spirit.

Of the thirteen sisters in our convent, six of us had en-joyed a camaraderie that contributed to our teaching and spiritual growth. Fall River had been a cloister where tra-dition died slowly. There the ghosts of nineteenth-century French nuns inhabited the crevices and interstices of the foundations.

In the Holy Rule it was stated that when a sister was transferred to another venue, she must go *sans éclat*—without ceremony. And so the life I'd been so eager to embrace at age eighteen was ending. I'd made my unequivocal decision. And I was leaving *without ceremony*.

Epilogue

I wish to express my appreciation to the Holy Union Sisters, to the memory of many who have passed on, and to those who remain friends. The Holy Union was my second home, and I am grateful for having lived with the virtuous women who brought joy to my life.

In writing this story I have described my memories of things past. Today repression is no longer countenanced as a path to sanctification. Some of the customs and regulations imposed upon us as novices and professed sisters were counterproductive and were, I think, carryovers from a medieval concept of righteousness. The superiors who came here from France had been imbued with a kind of Jansenism, and they handed down their beliefs to another generation of American novice mistresses who then trained American girls.

As young aspirants to the religious life in the fifties—many of us fresh out of high school, malleable and impressionable—cloistered without access to reading material or media, we were subject to indoctrination.

In my story I have described the change in atmosphere following the The Second Vatican Council and the implementation of reforms that led to saner and healthier lives for all of us working in the apostolate.

I tried to be a good religious during my years in Holy Union. When I began to study theology at Fordham and read some of the works of the European theologians, I found myself pulled in another direction.

In studying religion I lost my faith, and today I do not subscribe to Catholicism or to any other religion. It is my hope that no one is shocked by this revelation, for we all must follow our insights. I remember the quote my father told me years ago by Polonius in Hamlet:

"To thine own self be true."

CPSIA information can be obtained at www.ICGtesting.com
Printed in the USA
BVOW08s1504260116

434294BV00001B/16/P

9 781478 766186